The Heart of Man

The Heart of Man

⊕

Gerald Vann, O.P.

✣ Angelico Press

This Angelico Press edition
is a reprint of the book originally
published in 1945 by Longmans, Green & Co
Angelico Press reprint edition, 2020

For information, address:
Angelico Press
169 Monitor St.
Brooklyn, NY 11222
angelicopress.com

Unless otherwise indicated, Scripture quotations
are from the Douay-Rheims Bible

978-1-62138-669-8 (pbk)
978-1-62138-670-4 (cloth)
978-1-62138-67-1 (ebook)

Nihil Obstat: Fr. Daniel Callus, O.P., S.T.M., D. Phil.
Fr. Marcus Brocklehurst, O.P., S.T.L.

Imprimatur: Fr. Benedictus O'Driscoll, O.P.
Prior Provincialis Angliae, Londini, die 7a Iunii, 1943

Nihil Obstat: E. Hardwick, Ph.D., Censor Deputatis

Imprimatur: Leo, Episcopus Northantoniensis,
Northantoniae, die 13a Iulii, 1943

Cover design: Michael Schrauzer

For R. S.——FOR A BLESSING

CONTENTS

PART I

MAN THE LOVER

I

The Vision of the Whole

The heart of man is a hunger for the reality which lies about him and beyond him.

We think of our growth from child to man as a gradual passing from the receptive to the active, from dependence to independence: we are not fully man until we have ceased to cling to the skirts of a mother, the mother who bore us or a substitute for her, and begun to live our own life on our own initiative, to create for ourselves, to mould our lives and our world instead of allowing the world to mould us. We are right; but only half right. We can be independent and yet be dead in mind and spirit. Look at some of those who fulfil this description of the fullness of human life; it soon becomes apparent that there is something wrong.

There are men who have made their brilliant way in the world, answerable to no one but themselves, quick and assured of judgment, dominating the world about them and leaving the mark of their personality upon it through the events and conditions they have caused; but you find they have gained and used power pitilessly, they have treated men and things as mere utilities, brutally, and so at the end they are poorer than the poorest of their servants because they are completely alone. Loneliness is the stuff of hell; it is a big price to pay for power and glory.

But this is not primarily a moral question; it is not only the ruthless and brutal who pay the price. It is true that human growth means growth in independence, the emergence of the individual; but we of the modern age and the Western world are apt to think that it means nothing more; and if we do that we neglect something that lies at the core of our being. Pan is dead to us—not the wayward satyr but the great god in whom all things are one. Christians believe indeed that there is a God in whom "all things live and move and have their being," but it is easy in a world that prizes only the practical to forget what the belief implies. If we do, in fact, forget, we are doing two things: we are reducing human nature to a fraction of itself, and we are thereby condemning ourselves to eventual death of soul.

The human heart is a hunger for what lies beyond it. We of the Western world of today pride ourselves on our achievements as makers; we think of our civilization as being the most productive the world has ever seen. Perhaps we do not sufficiently reflect on the somber fact that whereas we regard the everyday products, the pots and pans, of other civilizations as things of beauty, our own works of art are so rare that we guard them jealously in special buildings reserved for them. It is no sufficient explanation to blame machinery; there are in fact beautiful things which have been produced by the use of machinery. The reason must lie deeper; in the soul.

There are two classes of human being whom we regard as not having reached the fullness of human stature even though we do admire their art-works: the primitive and the child. We can learn from them. They are both undeveloped, certainly, along the line of individuality and independence. But they have something which our civilization seems very largely to have lost. You will find children absorbed in conversation with animals, flowers, dolls, on a footing of intimacy and equality; you will find in the myths and fairy tales which enshrine primitive wisdom the same sharing of life between man and the rest of creation.

And if you should be tempted to feel that all this, though perhaps very charming, can rest on no basis of solid fact, you can find justification for it in the wisdom of the greatest minds of history or in the most modern discoveries of science. For the latter have shown us how, beneath the superficial differences of things, there is the same underlying stuff of reality: so that as the members of a family are one through the blood tie which binds them together, so the whole family of diverse beings is one through the unity of the ultimate physical elements which compose them. And philosophy too, which can take us so much further and deeper than physical science, tells us in its turn of the unity of the manifold: a unity which comes not only from an identity of material but from the fact that all things come as an ordered whole from a single source and march together to a single end, living in and expressing the fecundity of a single life.

But if we can see and accept that unity of the manifold with our minds, what is it that separates us from the child and the primitive? It is the abyss that lies between reason and vision, between knowledge *about* things and immediate perception *of* things. The child knows practically nothing about its kitten or its teddy-bear, but it knows them in a way that most grown-ups can never do. Partly this is a question of sense-knowledge: of bothering to stop and be conscious of color and shape and texture, of the smell and feel of things which to the adult are so familiar that he never looks at them. But that difference is not always verified; and, in any case, there is more than that. The gourmet is thoroughly aware of taste and smell and texture; to that extent he is a better man by far than the gourmand whose awareness stops short at quantity. Yet at the deepest level both may, in fact, be living the same kind of life; both may equally be standing over against objects which they covet as objects, as means to pleasure, just as the ruthless industrial magnate may stand over against the men he uses simply as means to profit. The child-life is in this respect a different *kind* of life altogether; and it is when this child-life is destroyed in us that we reduce our nature to a fragment of itself and condemn it to death.

Perhaps we shall see the meaning of the child-life most clearly if we think of the human experience which above all has power to turn the most mature and independent man back again, if only for an occasional fleeting moment, into a child. We talk about falling *in* love: it is one of the splendors of our language. No doubt the phrase has fallen on evil days, like so many others; it is often used to signify no more than a superficial excitement of the senses in which the personality as a whole has little part. But we know a reality far greater than this; and when two human beings are deeply and wholly bound to one another by love, then, indeed, love is not something which exists in them so much as something in which they exist.

They may or may not know a great deal about each other; what they do realize most certainly is that they know one another in a way that cannot be put down in words. You can say, "I know that he is this and this and this," but when you have exhausted all the qualities and characteristics, you have not expressed him. Love-knowledge is of a different kind from the knowledge that reason brings us. The two can, indeed, appear in contradiction. Reason may say, "I know that we are two"; love will say, "I know our oneness." (But the contradiction, if real, at any rate need not be final; to that point we return later on.)

The verdicts are different because their settings are so different as to change the meaning of the word "we." To the eye of the practical man and the scientist, the man and the woman are two distinct objects whose boundaries are clearly defined; they can look out from the fortress of their selfhood, can stretch out their hands to one another, can communicate, can share a great deal of what they have; they cannot share what they are, the two beings cannot fuse. This is the world of rational maturity. The world of the child is very different. The boundaries are no longer fixed and clear; the distinctness of objects from each other is hardly perceived; the self is not experienced as a subject standing over against a number of different objects; rather there is the apprehension of a single reality which in fact enfolds subject and object alike, but which is not so differentiated to the mind of the child. Similarly we are told of primitive peoples that consciousness of individuality has not fully emerged to replace the consciousness of the life of the race; and the life of man itself is seen not as standing out in contrast to the rest of creation but as identified with it.

The "we" of reason, then, means just two numerically distinct objects; and the two cannot fuse into one without loss of identity. But the "we" of love does not mean just two numerically distinct objects. The lovers must, indeed, live their lives in the realm of reason; they must be continually for one another objects of thought, of desire, of devotion and service; but there are moments when the sense of separateness disappears like a veil drawn aside and is replaced by a sense of oneness, and then there are not two things in whom love exists, but one thing which exists in love.

There are intimations of the same thing in the way in which places can cast a spell over us and become, as we say, a part of us. Poet and artist seem to know something of the same thing when they become possessed of the vision they will express in words or paint or stone. There is, as we shall have occasion to consider later, such a thing as being possessed by evil, which means living not in love but in hate...

Do these things seem very strange to us? Yet once, before reason emerged and took command in us, they must have been our life. They must still be so unless we want to reduce our nature to a fragment. We cannot live by reason alone. The heart of man is a hunger not to have reality but to be reality. It is difficult to exaggerate the greatness of reason; the reasoning mind can "become in a manner all things," and as it establishes more and more its mastery over nature, it finds more and more things that it can do; but though it become all things, they remain things, in separateness, and though it can master nature, it is not to a master that nature will reveal herself. If man is master and nothing more, he is doomed to misery in the midst of his greatness because he is doomed to remain alone.

Is this hard to believe? It was said of Napoleon that he made one wonder whether sovereigns could have a neighbor. But the king can exalt the beggar-maid? No doubt, but he cannot live in love with her unless he first clothe his own soul in rags, that she may exalt him. Even so, kings may consort together? Perhaps, but with reserve; for they have great possessions and will be jealous of them and suspicious of designs upon them. Reason can give us great possessions, can give us, indeed, the length and breadth and height and depth of the world; but that is not enough to make us happy. I want to have; but much more, I want to be.

Men of insight have remarked how modern people seem to lack the ties that bind together the members of simpler societies and are always more or less at war with one another, suspicious of one another, afraid of one another, always competing with one another. Then there comes the major crisis of war and they forget to be competitive and suspicious and remember again that they are brothers.

Why cannot they do in peace what they do in war? We shall have to discuss the ultimate answer in the following chapter; but here, surely, is the immediate one. They accept the idea of a social life based on competition (which therefore leads to avarice, envy, jealousy, war) in so far as they think of life itself in terms of having—having things, having persons, having power. Even virtues—prudence, justice, generosity—can be thought of as things to be possessed. But the desire to have can quickly become in practice the desire to have more and more; and then the desire to have more than others or to have what others have. There is such a thing as envy or jealousy even of "another's spiritual good." Are we then to condemn the desire to have? No; it is the driving force behind the growth to individuality. But when there is this and nothing more, then you get envy and enmity and the stunted heart; and the hunger of man finds an unnatural outlet in hatred and destruction.

There is the man of vision and there is the man of power—we might say there is the child and the man—but when human life is lived in its fullness, these two are one. Life follows a double direction: to individual independence and power, and to the sense of oneness with reality; these two ways may seem to be opposed, but they cannot be really opposed if we are living with the whole of our being and not just with a fragment of it. Take them apart and make either of them the whole of life, and then, indeed, there is contradiction; and the chosen fragment itself turns from life into decay and death. Put them together, and they complete and therefore vitalize one another.

Let us return for a moment to the man of power. We are familiar enough with the theme of the millionaire or the dictator who, in public, is always the great man, hard, hated and unhappy, but who can find a few fleeting moments of happiness with the one human being he really loves and with whom he can be himself. Precisely; it is only in those few moments that he is *himself*, and if it were not for them, he would not be a self at all. To gain the whole world by power methods is to lose one's own soul. In the arms of the woman he loves, even the dictator can be happy for a moment because for a moment he can be a child. But his life is thus an endless tension which is never resolved: he is now a man and now a child: is it ever possible to be both at once?

We might learn of the simplest craftsman a parable. We all know the difference between the carpenter who is really an artist and the man who can knock a bookcase together if he needs one. There is no doubt which of the two is master and maker; you watch with admiration the almost miraculous obedience of tool and material to the craftsman's will. But you notice that it is not he who asserts with every gesture his will to dominate; it is the hedge-carpenter who wrenches and forces and blusters and drives the wood to obey him against the grain. There is no great art without reverence. The real carpenter has great technical knowledge of material and tools; but the bungler might conceivably have that and still be a bungler. The real carpenter has something much more; he has the feel of wood, the knowledge of its demands is in his fingers; and so the work is smooth and satisfying and lovely because he works with the reverence that comes of love.

8

Apply this to any form of making, apply it to the way men treat animals they have care of, apply it to the relationship of men with men; always it is the lover and servant who is most the master and who seems to have magic spells at his command. And what do we mean by love and reverence and service here but a sense of kinship and unity? So that if we want to be wholly masters, we must be one not with this or that kind of thing merely, but with the whole world. Therefore, accept your destiny of greatness with both hands; learn to be a master; set about encompassing the vastnesses of reality; but remember that reality is not a nettle to be grasped, or a fruit to be plucked and eaten, but a bride to be wooed.

It is time to begin to talk about the vision of the Whole.

I sit at my table. It is not a thing of great beauty. The wood is deal, the workmanship undistinguished. If I go out, I shall see uglier things, a mongrel dog, a strident guttersnipe, repulsive men and women. Am I to love and reverence and establish my kinship with these?

We live in a scientifically minded age, and our ideal is too exclusively the man of power. So the artist does us an immense service when he tells us to stop treating things as means and utilities for a moment and to look at them and love their beauty. But if he in his turn has no use for the dull and the undistinguished we must look for a further guide; aesthetic sensibility by itself will not make us whole.

We live in a scientifically minded age, not because of the greatness of the conquests of science in our days (for they might have happened in an age which was not scientifically minded), but because so many people who are not themselves scientists, and a certain number still who are, believe what the great majority of scientists believed fifty years ago: that if there is anything that science cannot tell us about, nothing else can tell us about it either, for the simple reason that it is not there. So they cling to the belief that science can guide us into a better and happier world—or at least that if science cannot, nothing else can.

It is a strange belief on the face of it. There are so many things it must regard as nonexistent which we know perfectly well to exist. In the second place, you cannot guide someone unless you know where he wants to go. Science has increased our knowledge enormously; but the increase is either in the realm of "how" or answers only immediate questions "why." If we want to heal humanity, science can tell us how; if we want to destroy humanity, science can tell us how; but on what grounds can it tell us which of the two to do? If we want to know why certain things behave in certain ways in certain circumstances, science can tell us why; but it cannot tell us why the things exist at all; it cannot tell us why there is such a thing as being; and therefore it cannot answer the question of the ultimate "whither." We must go elsewhere. If we are not determined to maim and diminish the mind by refusing to listen to anything but science, we shall learn more. It is reasonable to refuse to accept the unreasonable; but it is very unreasonable to refuse without question to accept the nonscientific.

The ultimate questions why and whither are not scientific questions because they are not questions of empirically observable fact; but that does not mean that there is no answer to them. We must choose; either we must believe that the universe is ultimately unintelligible because science cannot explain it; or we must accept an explanation which does make the universe intelligible but which is not supplied by science. There is an intelligible answer; and there is only one. All the things that we know are fleeting; they come to be and they pass away. They do not exist necessarily therefore; they can either be or not be. And this is the same as saying that they do not exist of themselves; they exist at all only because they have received existence from something else. And ultimately, therefore, that something else must be a thing that does exist of itself; and because it exists of itself it is rightly called Being Itself—not something that has existence, but something that is existence.

And if we go on to recognize the presence of design and order in the universe, we shall recognize that this Being is not an It but a He; and then we may be ready to learn more about Him from religion. We of the modern West are the only people in the whole history of the world who have refused to find an explanation of the universe in a divine mind and will; and it is worth wondering whether perhaps that refusal is not at the root of the chaos and misery in which we find ourselves. Without a sense of ultimate purpose, without intelligible answer to the ultimate why and whither, what else could we expect?

The conviction that science is all dies hard. But we may take comfort from the fact that a dissenting voice and a powerful one has been heard from within the camp of science itself. Psychology is sometimes said to have shown that God is simply a creature of the human mind, an expression of its desires and dreams, an enlarged and glorified version of the human father. This is far from being an accurate statement of the case. No doubt it is more or less true of the position adopted by Freud; but Freud, though a genius at his own line of investigation, was certainly not a great thinker, and when he attempted to draw from his psychological discoveries conclusions which went beyond the domain of psychology, he was often wild and sometimes puerile. Freud did regard religion as a disease of the mind.

But with Jung the case is very different. Though he started by accepting Freud's position in this respect, he came more and more to the contrary view that absence of religion was the root cause of all diseases of the mind. That is a statement of observed fact; it does not prove that God exists. Psychology cannot prove that religious beliefs are valid, any more than it can prove that philosophical principles are true. But it can help belief so to say from outside. Can we, unless we are prepared to acquiesce despairingly in the idea that the universe is ultimately unintelligible, believe that religion is a psychological necessity and at the same time a falsehood, a pure figment of man's mind? But there is more than that. To be acquainted with traditional Christian theology and then to read the works of Jung is to be startled at every turn by the way in which the two dovetail or run parallel. The hunger for the infinite which alone can fill the human heart, the longing for spiritual rebirth, the felt need for the healing and turning to good of the "dark shadow" within the self, the need of integration, of being made whole—all these things are both psychological fact and religious truth; psychology, therefore, confirming belief in religious doctrine, and religion fulfilling the needs and desires which psychology empirically reveals.

Jung's immense learning enabled him to show how the myths of all the peoples of the world express in different, though indeed startlingly similar, ways the same deep-rooted desires, so that it is true to say of them that they enshrine not the particular beliefs of a particular race so much as the age-old dreams of humanity as such. This very fact is sometimes taken as a proof that Christian beliefs are no truer, no more "real," than any other religious myth. But it is possible to draw an opposite conclusion. Accept for a moment the Christian position; in the book of Genesis we are shown the first human beings receiving an assurance that eventually those very desires we have been considering will be fulfilled, and be fulfilled through the agency of a particular Man. Is it then surprising that we should find this original promise reappearing, in different dress and often in distorted form, among the peoples of the world? On the contrary, it would be surprising and indeed inexplicable if we did not; for it would mean that a promise on which the deepest desires of man were set had been discarded as unimportant.

More than that. Accept again, for a moment, the Christian belief in the goodness of God the Creator; is it conceivable that there should not be a correspondence between man's deepest desires and his actual destiny? Is it conceivable that this God should have made a nature which of itself is a hunger for these things, and should then have refused them to it? But if there is, in fact, such a correspondence, if heaven and wholeness and the fulfilling of the heart are both dream and destiny, then we must surely expect that, even where the promise of the reality has been forgotten or distorted, the reality of the dream will remain; we shall expect the peoples of the whole earth to find similar symbols to express the reality, even though to a greater or less extent they have forgotten that it is a reality.

Psychology of itself can neither prove nor disprove the validity of religious belief. But there is another way in which it has indirectly helped us, by demonstrating from within the realm of science itself that we cannot live by science alone. One of the things which Jung has made most clear is the fact that the personality has not one function but four; is not reason merely but feeling, sensation, intuition as well. It can thus, if the arguments of reason leave us cold, lead us on to explore other ways to reality.

There have been men and women—and a vast multitude of them, of every race and age, of every type of temperament, of every kind of mental stature from unlettered peasant to the greatest minds in history—who have claimed not only to have known about God but to have known Him. It is very difficult to dismiss them all as neurotic victims of hallucination without doing violence to reason. For the thing that strikes one about so many of them is precisely their realness, their homely common sense and practical ability. If they are so obviously real in themselves, their claim to have found Reality is worth considering.

They are valuable bridgemakers; they tell us from personal experience that the dreams which psychology expounds to us and the reality which religion proclaims do, in fact, correspond; they tell us from experience that we do, in fact, inhabit an intelligible and not an unintelligible world. They tell us—what psychology may have led us to expect or at least to hope for, what philosophy may have convinced us of in some degree, what religion has taught with assurance— that beyond and above the world (to speak in spatial metaphors) there is an Infinite Perfect, untouched by the fleetingness of time and change, whom the philosophers therefore call the Absolute; but they go on to say that the Infinite is yet not unattainable by the spirit of man; dwelling in light inaccessible He is yet present within the world that He has made and within every creature in it; but within the creature man He can dwell in a special sense, not by any power of human nature itself but by His own gift, as object of knowledge and love and in a union, therefore, like the union of lovers; and they tell us, finally, that it is when this union is achieved that we are made whole, when we are one with this all-embracing Reality that our desire to be is completely fulfilled and our loneliness for ever healed.

If we are made one with this One we are reborn, and can find earth a heaven even though hell lies about us.[1] I sit at my uninteresting table, I meet the uninteresting dog and child and man, but they need not be uninteresting now. "He sees God aright who sees Him in all things; we are *all* one in that One." You know that feeling—something akin, perhaps, to the sense of the holy—with which we touch things or even revisit places closely bound up with someone we deeply love. The personality can project itself upon the things it touches, the house it lives in, the words it uses; they take on a being and a value beyond themselves. But in Him are *all* things; and if we love Him all things are holy. The saint kisses the leper: a theatrical gesture, a neurotic aberration? No, an affirmation, forced by pride and pity from the depths of the soul, that this is the temple of God and my brother. The saint preaches to the birds and calls the moon his sister; it is because he knows they sing the same song as he, and it is a song we must sing with them or not at all, for it is the *Laudes Creaturarum,* the song of the spheres; it is because we are all one in the One, and if we forget our oneness, we isolate and kill ourselves; it is because we are responsible for one another, and if we deny our responsibility, we deny our destiny.

When the priest and the Levite saw the naked wounded man by the wayside and passed by, they lessened themselves, the little hard shell of their selfhood contracted still further

---

[1] A fuller discussion of the meaning and necessity of rebirth follows in Chapter II.

about them; but the Samaritan who befriended him was enlarged by the flow of life and power that passed between them (for to give life lovingly is always also to receive it) and was himself made whole. What a lot we lose if we attempt to live by science alone and to regard poetry and prayer not as roads to reality but as a parlor game and a mental disease. It is only poetic justice when we ourselves end up in a mental home. It is also the logical conclusion; for madness is complete inability to communicate, complete isolation, and isolation is precisely the wages of this sin.

Let us meditate on a story told by a Persian poet:

> The lover knocks at the door of the Beloved, and a voice replies from within: Who is there? It is I, he said; and the voice replied: There is no room for thee and me in this house. And the door remained shut. Then the lover retired to the desert and fasted and prayed in solitude. After a year he came back, and knocked once more at the door. Once more the voice asked: Who is there? He replied: It is thyself. And the door opened to him.[2]

We cannot live without reason. Science can tell us much about things that we need to know; philosophy can tell us much that we need to know still more. But of itself all this knowledge is a having, not a being; it will not by itself satisfy the hunger of the heart; it will not of itself make us whole. It will not reveal to us the heart of things. Poetry may lead us to the heart of things; but perhaps as we read we may stop short at beauty, and have no use for the halt and the blind and the lame. The love of man and woman for one another can

---

[2] Quoted in H. Bremond, *Prayer and Poetry,* 141.

16

lead them to the heart of things; yet in itself it has an exclusiveness which may make them impatient with the call of the outer world. The love of art and nature may be no more than a self-glorification unless there is the love of humanity too. But the love of humanity can be a fantasy and a deception, compatible with cruelty to individual men and women—the rich philanthropist who lives on sweated labor, the condescending social worker, the builder of new social orders which involve the unpitying liquidation of the old—unless, beneath the perhaps unattractive, perhaps repulsive and exasperating surface, is sensed the presence and love of Infinite Being and Infinite Beauty, so that "It is thyself" can be said to the whole of the manifold and to every part of it, because it is said primarily to the abiding Presence, within the manifold, of the One.

The table may be a poor thing, but it is wood; and we know the symbolism of the Tree of Life, we know that by the touch of a Body on the rood-tree the tree is blessed, we know that where the pagans sensed the presence of the dryad of the tree there is in fact the reality of the omnipresent One. The dog may be a poor thing; but if it is, it can stand as a symbol (as it is indeed a part) of the pain of the world for which we are all in part responsible; and because it, in its turn, is not deserted by the Father, we may find that through its bruises, too, we are healed. The human being may seem uninteresting or repulsive, and that again may be our fault; but in addition there is here a greater mystery, for beneath the externals there may lie hidden a grandeur that is more than human—and if there is not, there is a void the very tragedy of which should compel our love.

It is terrifyingly hard to learn all this. No one in his senses would say that the way to wholeness is easy. It is easy to fall in love with a beautiful thing or person; but those who have seen the Whole have warned us precisely against the dangers of a partial vision, the sort of vision that closes its eyes to the ugly, the silly, the dull. The love of the beauty of this and that can be the lotus-flower that lulls us to forgetfulness of the One, of whom they are only a partial mirroring; and so we may find that we are clutching only at a shadow and that the heart even of the things we love escapes us because we see them as mirroring not the Infinite Love and Beauty, but ourselves.

It is hard to learn to say, "It is thyself." There are the two desires that drive us: the desire to be reality, the desire to be the self. Love in a sense is a dependence; and we want to be independent, at least to retain something for ourselves. So, perhaps, we find ourselves, even against our will, throwing open our hearts, saying, "I love and I worship," and yet keeping back the inner secret core of the self—terrified that if we lose that, we lose ourselves. Of God especially there is this fear: If I let Him take all, I shall cease to be myself; and sometimes, because of the fear, there is the temptation to take refuge in the externals of religion, to lead the ordinary pedestrian good life, when we might be soaring like the eagle in the infinite sky. But the inexorable paradox rings down the ages, and if we are not careful it will sometimes sweep like a mighty wind through the cozy house we have built: He that loseth his life shall find it. If we want to be all reality, we must first have felt that we are nothing. If we want to say, "I am myself," we must first have learnt to say, "It is thou." There is an apparent contradiction between the lover and the master, between the man of vision and the man of power; but it will be real and irremediable unless we are willing to solve it by dying and being reborn. Unless the grain of wheat, falling into the ground, die, itself remaineth *alone*...

18

The fear is first of all a moral fear: I want to keep my own will. Can the free man, precisely as free, obey? But a deeper fear lies underneath: I want to keep my own identity. Can the lover, precisely as lover, be his own master? Can it be an "I" that says, "It is thyself"? For the first, ask the man who is living in love whether in doing the other's will he is not of necessity doing his own; ask the Man who said, "My meat is to do the will of Him that sent me." It is not the free man who cannot obey; on the contrary, it is only the free man who can obey. To respond as an automaton, to be forced into compliance like a slave, this is not obedience. To carry out another's will freely but with reluctance is truly obedience, but not fully freedom. To carry out another's will because by the power of love that will *is* your own: that is the perfect work in which freedom and obedience are wholly fused.

If, then, there is no loss of freedom, how can there be loss of identity? Ask the lovers again, of God and of men alike: do they not all tell us, so far as they can tell the inexpressible, that there is no loss but an immense enhancement of being: that if "I" becomes "Thou" it is not by losing the real self but by finding it? What needs to die is not the real self but the false: the self that tries to think it is whole and complete when, in fact, it is fragmentary. What needs to die is not love of self but self-love. "I live, now not I, but Christ liveth in me"—and that is why *I* live. Note another thing that St. Paul also said, "I can do all things in Him who strengtheneth me." It is in holiness (or wholeness, the same thing) that the lover-master contradiction is fully resolved. "I live, now not I"— that is the lover, saying, "It is thyself"; "I can do all things"— that is the master.

But note also that it is love and only love which makes the two compatible; the second phrase itself is in two parts, "I

19

can do all things" (that is the man) "in him who strengtheneth me" (that is the child). We begin as children; we go on, unless we are very fortunate, to forget our childhood and become merely men, or to cling to our childhood dependence and fail to be men; so we have to go on and fight for our fullness until we are both child and man. But that is not accurately said either; for it is not a question of a juxtaposition of two beings but of one single being. And can love really achieve this? We have already seen the answer in little in the carpenter; look now for the full answer to the saints.

You want independence, you want to be master and maker, you want power, you want to be great: you are right, it is your destiny. But who is powerful, the man who can evict a thousand villagers from their homes or throw a million soldiers into the field and destroy a nation, or the man who can make a single human being give him his whole heart? Be the first if you will: you will intoxicate yourself, no doubt, with your greatness and forget or never notice that it is not you at all that wields the power. Posterity will not fail to notice; and, indeed, before you are dead they will be analyzing you as a specimen and explaining precisely the gods— the lusterless sub-human gods—whose lackey you were. You will have seen yourself as the master of millions; they will know you as a man who never even had the sense to master his own unconscious urges. You will have thought yourself lord of the world; they will know you as an outcast, unable to win a glance from a single heart, unable to find a single friend unless, perhaps, it were a dog—and even the dog would, no doubt, have learnt only to fawn.

It is the saints who are independent: they have mastered themselves and are whole; they do what they like and no man can stop them, for they laugh at terror and torture, having

20

nothing to lose. It is the saints who have power: they need not rely on bribery or blackmail or bayonets, for their power is really theirs, within them, and it is simply by being themselves that they sway the world. When the lions lick the feet of Paulinus in the Roman arena, when Laurence makes fun of himself on the gridiron, when thousands flock to the confessional of the illiterate Curé at Ars, when millions love and honor Bernadette because she was humble, when people lose their hearts to the saints not for what they do but for what they are, because in themselves they are real, in themselves they are lovely—that is power. Real power is like real happiness: you find it when you have stopped looking for it because you have found something even more important to do. That is why real power is never spoilt but goes on growing through the ages: whereas in far less than a lifetime the power of the tinpot Caesar is likely to decay.

Real power is to the lover. That is why it is idle to hope or work for a new world, a league of nations, unless we are ready or at least trying to be ready to kiss the leper: not the priest or the Levite but only the Samaritan can rebuild the world.

To say that between man as master and man as lover there is no contradiction is not to say that there is no tension. On the contrary. That is why the way to wholeness is so hard. Just how deep and dangerous the tension is, we shall have to examine later. But even though we may never fully resolve the tension in ourselves, it is something to know that our destiny lies in solving it and that it can eventually be solved.

What have we to do? We have to learn not to treat things merely as means; we have to learn to be lover-masters and not merely to tyrannize over externals. Utilitarianism is always shallow. Perhaps it is by an inescapable logical necessity that, if we start by turning things into mere means to our pleasure or profit, we finish by turning means into ends; we make science a leader instead of a servant, and so we condemn ourselves to chaos or at best to living exclusively on the surface of life.

Every creature that exists, exists first of all in its own right. Its destiny may be to serve some other creature greater than itself, but that service does not comprehend its destiny. The ultimate purpose of all creatures is to sing to God. Therefore, whenever I try to say of anything, "This is wholly mine and wholly for me," I do violence to the thing as well as to myself. Yet that is what all the time we are tempted to do. We are always being tempted to possess ourselves of things, to possess ourselves of persons, even to possess ourselves of knowledge. Descartes thought that the supreme purpose of knowledge was to make us masters of nature; there have been more modern advertisements proclaiming knowledge as a paying investment. That way true wisdom will escape us. We might learn from the great scientists themselves—for it is not they, it is their ignorant camp-followers who are utilitarians. We might learn from the great philosophers, who know that wisdom is a mistress who must be wooed in silence and humility. We might learn from the saints, who worship the Truth. Knowledge is power, yes; but before we can use the power with safety we must worship. So with things, and still more with persons. First you must look for them as things in themselves, first you must see and love; then you can use them with impunity and without violence because you will be using them with love.

Consider the lilies of the field. We live in a world which teaches us to value things only for their utility to ourselves.

The lilies are of utility to M. Coty. The grass is of utility to the farmer, the tree to the timber merchant, stone to the contractor, the sky to Imperial Airways and the sea to Grimsby. All this is very well; but how appalling if this is all. Man the *entrepreneur*—which being interpreted is, so rightly, the undertaker. First you must *consider* the lilies of the field, and see that not even Solomon in all his glory (let alone yourself) is arrayed as one of these. But there is something which must come before that—not prior in time, perhaps, but infinitely in importance—the thing beside which nothing else matters, lest you look for a lily and find a lotus-flower. You will not see the manifold aright unless you have found the One.

Those who know by experience tell us what we must do. *Noli foras ire*, said Augustine; leave for a time every day the bustle of the street and the forum, refuse the mind and imagination their extravagance, quieten sense and desire, banish anxiety and care if only for a moment, and make things still.

> In a dark night,
> With anxious love inflamed,
> O happy lot!
> Forth unobserved I went,
> My house being now at rest.
>
> In that happy night,
> In secret, seen of none,
> Seeing nought myself,
> Without other light or guide
> Save that which in my heart was burning.
>
> That light guided me,
> More surely than the noonday sun,
> To the place where He was waiting for me...
>
> And I caressed Him, and the waving
> Of the cedars fanned Him.

23

To set the house at rest; it is more than a quiet of the mind, as we shall see, but it is, in any case, only a beginning. The journey is a very long one, and it is easy to be discouraged just as in the later stages it is easy to be frightened. And all the time, all the time, we are being pulled the other way. But on the other way lies disintegration; it is faith that makes us whole if day by day we go doggedly on.

Then we shall be able to return to the lilies and find our eyes fully opened. We shall have something much more than an aesthetic sense. We shall see their beauty indeed, and shall rejoice; but we shall see what lies beyond and yet within them, and then we shall know our kinship with the sun and the stars. We shall know, too, our kinship with the halt and the lame, the dull and the stupid, the leper. Then, finally, we shall be whole.

But whole only in principle, this side the grave. To have the root of the matter in us is only to be at the beginning. To have solved a contradiction in principle is not necessarily to have resolved a tension in practice. There is no life for the heart here on earth without hunger; if we were ever to discover that we were no longer hungry, we should be dead, however solid and active our bodies remained.

For first of all we can never find God in His fullness; it is only hereafter that we can see Him as He is. Then the same is true of our love of the world and of man: if there are those rare moments of ecstasy when there seems nothing left to desire, still they are evanescent, we return to the pedestrian self, and the completeness of union for ever eludes us. Then there is the tension between the two worlds, the wicket swings "between the Unseen and Seen"; to say "I love you in God" may be an insult to you, as meaning that I do not see you and love you (as God does) for yourself; and to say simply "I love you" may be an insult to God, as meaning that when I see you I deify you—I cannot remember that you are His. And then, behind all this, the greatest tension of all persists until we are perfect; between the self that is learning to be the world and the self that wants to have the world; for between these also the wicket swings as long as the breath of evil can touch us. To have glimpsed the vision of the Whole is the essential, but it is not the same as to be fully whole. We must exorcize the devil before we can see God.

Is it necessary to remind ourselves of an obvious rider: that laughter is the frequent complement of love? To gaze mournfully at the funny is irreverent. We are all a family, and you cannot have family life without humor. There are some people who never laugh at the giraffe or the hippopotamus. But then there are some people who never even laugh at themselves. Perhaps it is unkind to say that; perhaps they cry. (But one has the feeling that the people who cry are not the people who need to, or at least who need to most.) We are given the giraffe and the hippo to keep us young of heart; for it is only as children that we can receive of God's fullness, only as children that we can become the world.

But we cannot become all this without becoming men. So, as man and child together, we shall be able without doing them violence to be masters of the things whose destiny it is to serve; we shall be able to be makers without doing violence to our material or destroying our vision; we shall be able to use reason and science without condemning ourselves to isolation; we shall be able to use power without danger of self-destruction; because to everything in its particularity and to Him who is All in all we shall have learnt to say, "It is thyself."

II

The Vision
of Good and Evil

Only a fool could deny the fact of sin, though we may choose to call it by another name. In the beginning, we are told, God planted a garden, and set therein the man He had made, to dress it and keep it; and He walked with him in the garden in the cool of the evening. Let us not argue for the moment about whether we should speak of the first man or the first men, or to what extent we must treat with scientific literalness the primitive Semitic symbolism of the Genesis story.[1] The essential thing conveyed is simple. It is also extraordinarily compelling, not only because it corresponds with the age-old dreams of humanity, but also because it describes the ruthless facts of humanity. Already, in the depicting of this life of paradise, we can see the possibility of what we now are.

In the beginning man was made. The men of prayer are fond of telling us that we are a spark of the eternal, infinite fire; the spark is thrown off and there is duality, and yet the spark cannot exist outside the fire; the heart of man is a hunger to be one with God, and yet God is wholly other.

Then God said of man, "Let him have dominion over the fishes of the sea and the fowls of the air and the beasts and the

[1] Cf. Appendix.

whole earth"—let him be man the master. God put him in the garden to dress it and keep it—let him be man the maker. But in the cool of the evening He walked with him in the garden—and then he was not man the master and maker, but a child. Here in this double duality, one and yet other, man and yet child, lies the possibility of the tensions we have been considering.

What turned the possibility into fact? The serpent told the woman, "In what day soever you shall eat of the tree of knowledge of good and evil your eyes shall be opened and you shall be as gods." To know is to have power over the known; to be as gods knowing good and evil is to be autonomous, to accept no master, to deny that truth and therefore goodness are absolute, and to claim the power to define them. Thus the primal sin is the sin of pride, of *superbia*: a "fall upwards," therefore, since it is the dependent attempting to be autonomous, the relative attempting to be absolute, man attempting to be God. But the attempt to liberate the man involves the death of the child: the sin consists in setting up the ego in the centre of the personality instead of God; the immediate effect is isolation, loneliness, which is the essence of hell, so that hell is not so much a punishment *for* sin as the immediate and inevitable result *of* sin.

Then from the isolation of the personality follows with equal inevitability a dislocation within the personality. It is a state of affairs we know only too well. Integrity means that the various elements in the personality work together and in hierarchy for the good of the whole. Remove the true centre and sovereign, and the hierarchy breaks down at every point; each element apes the original attempt at autonomy and goes its way, and there is civil war.

A further disorder follows: man loses his dominion over

the world. The dislocation of nature repeats the dislocation of man. As man is isolated from and at enmity with God and at the same time the battleground on which the elements within him go to war, so the rest of the world is isolated from man and at enmity with him and at the same time rent by violence and cruelty within itself. Here the darkness of mystery deepens. We know that God does not cause evil, and the men of prayer tell us that where ugliness and strife are, there is hell; we know that God intended man to have dominion over the animals; we know that, in fact, the ideal has been shattered, the design has gone awry.

Beyond that we can only speculate. Two things, however, seem to be clear. First, as it is at least reasonable to be led by the facts of experience to look for some force of evil in the world beyond (yet operative in) the evil initiated by individuals here and now—in other words, to explain the bias toward evil in the individual by reference to the continuing effects of an original sin whereby the human species fell—so also it is at least reasonable to be led by the facts of experience to look for a yet greater force of evil in the world, to accept the idea of a "mystery of iniquity," beyond and yet operative in the evil wrought by the human race. "The serpent tempted me and I did eat"—but it is not only to explain the primal sin of humanity that we may be led to accept the serpent as a fact. Earlier ages were familiar with the idea of diabolic possession, the enslavement of the human personality to an evil agency external to it. The scientific age dismissed the idea as a primitive superstition: in its eyes, the reality was nothing more than a form of mental disorder. Now we swing back again, and are more ready to listen to the psychologist who tells us that, on the contrary, mental disorder is a form of diabolic possession. There is evil abroad in the world which just cannot be explained in terms of human baseness; it will not be reduced to human terms, for so to explain it would be to explain it away.

And alas, it cannot be explained away. Just as there are times when the human heart is stilled by the sense of the holy in the presence of a person or an event, so there are times when it is stricken by the presence of a force of evil far greater than man, whether it be searching the cosmic problem of suffering, or watching a war, or gazing into itself. The heart of man is an abyss; there is room in it for infinity because in it there is an infinity of desire; and it cannot remain empty; the stark horror of an alien evil will inhabit it if it is not filled by the limitless ocean of the goodness of God. There is no reason to suppose that the serpent does not refer to an evil energy outside humanity; there is every reason to suppose that it does. And Catholic teaching does, in fact, tell us of spirits greater than man, intermediaries, therefore, between him and God, some of whom fell before him and so, instead of filling their appointed place in the harmony of creation, turn their giant power to the task of destroying it.

Do we find it difficult to understand how purely spiritual events could affect the animals and even the physical world? But we have seen a dog, by some unexplained sympathy, instantly reflecting its master's mood; the power of animals to sense "psychic" events or influences which escape us is well known; and are we being puerile or perhaps more scientific than we know when we say of two people who hate one another intensely that when they meet, the "air is electric"? Christ had power over the elements; there are evidences of the same power in the saints; there are other indications, though vague, of the power of the human spirit to influence its material environment for good or for evil—and to gauge the power of the spirit of evil, you would have, perhaps, to intensify the human spirit a million times.

However that may be, and whatever the precise history of the Fall of the world may be, at any rate (and this is the second point) we cannot absolve ourselves from all responsibility here and now. If fallen man is divinely healed as we believe, still his renewal and wholeness wait also upon his will, and must be earned by the sweat of his brow: not a moment of magic but a long and laborious process; and as in the beginning he fell, not in isolation but into isolation (for it was man in oneness with reality who fell), so he must be restored into that oneness, and it is he who must labor to restore the world to something of its integrity, for that task, too, waits upon his will. The whole of creation is in travail even until now; and as long as it is so, we have not fulfilled our task, we remain responsible.

But we must be whole before we can make whole. No wonder we cannot heal more than the fringe of animal nature—we have not yet banished hatred and bloodshed from among ourselves. It is no good expecting the world to become once again a garden unless we first learn again how to walk with God.

Unless ye become as little children... But the child is dead. And how, Nicodemus said to Him, "how can a man be born when he is old?" Jesus had elsewhere answered, "Unless the grain of wheat, falling into the ground, die, itself remaineth alone." The self that I have exalted to autonomy and set up in the centre of life and isolated: this must fall into the ground and die. The age-old dreams of humanity express just this in their symbols; and the symbols are made manifest and the dream fulfilled in the person of Christ. The Fall begins with the uprising of the self to autonomy, and is followed by the collapse of the personality into chaos. The restoration must reverse the process: only after we have gone down into the depths of self-knowledge and known the hell we had made for ourselves can we begin to rise again.

One of the men of prayer, William Law, tells us that Christ's greatest suffering was His entry into the eternal death that was man's fate, the last terror of the lost soul, that He might conquer it. And indeed, the last cry torn from His heart was a cry of isolation—"Why hast Thou forsaken me?" But what was done in and by Christ must be somehow relived by us if we would be made whole and so share in His victory and in its fruits. So here too, says the same mystic, we must with Him "go over the brook Cedron and sweat drops of sorrow"; for we shall never be truly religious if we have only known the "want of a Savior by hearsay." We must find and face our hell.

It should not be difficult to find it. When the master of the house finds his servants troublesome and rebellious and is too weak to control them, he sometimes consoles his pride by pretending not to notice that they are there. This is what reason does in its attempt at autonomy: it has lost control of the rest of the personality, and so it shuts its eyes to it and denies its existence. This seems to explain the shallowness of the Age of Enlightenment, of all but the greatest of the classicists. No doubt it explains also the bluster of the art that exalts humanity instead of worshipping God: it is always the man who is unsure of himself, the weakling, who blusters. But you cannot live forever on the surface; sooner or later there will be an explosion, the buried realities will burst forth, and their sojourn underground will not have improved them. Here we can surely say we speak what our eyes have witnessed. The humanist house of cards is about our ears; the underworld has broken forth and launched its Reign of Terror; and this time it is Reason and everything we call humane which is dragged away in the tumbril.

At this point there is a serious danger. It is so easy and so comforting to one's pride to feel righteous indignation over another's wickedness. And it is always the other man who is wicked. If that is the way we think, we can never be reborn. But suppose, as a matter of fact, that in a given case it *is* the other man: am I to feel guilty? If it were your brother, you would feel involved in his guilt—and we are all brothers. And more than that; if it were your brother, you would reproach yourself for not having prevented it; you would feel yourself responsible—and we are all brothers. We are each responsible for all; we are all one in the solidarity of sin. If we are living in love, it is a single life that in Donne's phrase "inter-inanimates" two souls; if we were all living in the Whole, it would be a single Presence inter-inanimating the world. And when we live not in love but in hate, not in God but in evil, then we work to make that evil more and more pervasive, to make *that* the energy that animates the world; we work for the world's disintegration and for the isolation of men—"Am I my brother's keeper?"; and as long as the devil is not cast out, as long as evil is abroad, we have failed and are responsible.

Do you think that the intense sense of sin that we find in the all but sinless saints is a pose? We take our part in a cosmic struggle; and we are the bearers—the conductors—of energies immensely greater than our own. "I live, now not I, but Christ": and what did Christ say? "*All* power is given to me in heaven and in earth." Is there anything that the wholly God-filled man could not do? And that is precisely our destiny: to wield the power of Christ, to heal the world in the power of Christ. *Instaurare omnia in Christo*, to restore all things—the motto of a recent Pope—that is our duty, and in so far as we fail to do it by failing to take and pass on, to the fullest limit of our capacity, the power of God, we are still to that extent in sin.

It is not only the horrors of evil that confront us, it is the horror of the sufferings of the innocent which evil brings about. Here, too, it is tempting to shut one's eyes, to say, "I didn't cause it and I detest the evil that did cause it, but I cannot cure it and I cannot bear to see it any more." And it is true that there comes a point beyond which one cannot see any more and the senses are mercifully numbed; but again we cannot shake off responsibility, for again it is we, in part, who are the cause. This cross, too, we must carry; it has its purpose. We must go with Christ over the brook Cedron. Why was the Word made flesh, why the agony and the cross and the dereliction, if not in order that the inconceivable might become fact, that the Infinite Perfect might weep and sweat drops of sorrow for the sufferings of men, and so bring them back by the only way possible to the deepest knowledge of His love and so to love Him, and to become once again children—themselves. The Word was made flesh that God might suffer with His servants.

Never think that this is all over; that it was God, indeed, who wept over Jerusalem, but that for our days there can be no tears. We can write the history of the life of Christ; but God has no history. What was done in and by the humanity of Christ was done in time; but it is God who acts and suffers through the humanity, and God is not in time. The tears were shed at a historical moment which is past, though it was not for that place and that moment only but for the whole past and future of the world that He wept. And just as each moment of the age-long process is equally present to the eternal "now," so, too, the sorrow that God suffers in the soul of Christ is not a distant memory but an eternal actuality. Did you think that God wept over Jerusalem but must be deaf to the cries of suffering that fill the whole world today? The Word was made flesh and dwelt amongst us that not a single cry or tear torn from the heart of humanity—yes, and the heart of nature, too—might be left unshared by the heart of God: and so we have seen His glory.

Can we now see ourselves? For if we can see both ourselves and His glory we shall no longer know the need of a Savior only by hearsay.

See, see how Christ's blood streams in the firmament!—it is the promise of renewal, but first there is the fall of all the bastions of pride. Before the baptism, the repentance. See how Christ's blood streams: it is my doing. See the agony of all the innocent: I am to blame. The sins of the world are my sins, for it is my world. (What a travesty to think religion means saving my little soul through my little good deeds and the rest of the world go hang.) Through fear, says St. Bernard, we come to the self-knowledge that is born of humility, and thence to the understanding of love. But to love is precisely to surrender the citadel of the autonomous self, to die therefore and be reborn. It was precisely when Francis had stripped himself of his possessions and gone naked from his house (naked as a new-born child) that he began to sing, "I am a king's son."

How must we strip and dethrone the pseudo-self? We have already seen in principle. It is simple to state, though it is so endlessly difficult to do. You have been pretending to be a king. The king commands whom and what he will, and the world waits upon his pleasure; the king's word is law. Very well, you must stop regarding things as your creatures, and you must obey the law of absolute truth. Blessed are the poor in spirit... It is a question both of mind and of will.

Take the will first. The Christian child is taught that there are seven "capital vices"; seven principal ways in which the instincts find not a self-creative and unitive mode of expression, but an outlet that drives the personality further and further into isolation and darkness: pride (*superbia*, the primal sin), covetousness, lust and gluttony, anger, envy, sloth. They are logically connected. Pride establishes the autonomous self as the centre and lord of the world; it follows inevitably that from that point of vantage it can view things only as means to its pleasure or profit, and the deep-rooted instinct of desire and love is expressed in brutal and rapacious grasping. You see something lovely; you must seize it and have it for your own; and you hide it away, you build a great fence about your property, lest anyone else should lay hands upon it. The two deep instincts of self-preservation and reproduction in particular are turned to the service of the pseudo-self, avaricious, grasping, utilizing; beauty not a queen in her own right but a serf to your pleasures.

Then, having built your fence and barred your gates, you are never at rest; your possessions are a millstone round your neck because you are forever terrified of losing them; you become care-worn. You become hard-hearted also, and men are no longer your brothers, the family life is destroyed; suspicion and fear turn love into anger and hatred, and you envy other men for what they have and what, therefore, because they have it, escapes you. Your life takes on all the characteristics of Hobbes's "state of nature"; and finally, worn out by care and anxiety and tumult, you sink into sloth—not laziness and inactivity, but that state in which the spirit is smothered and lacks even the desire to come back to life because it has forgotten what life is. The young man in the Gospel "went away sorrowful because he had great possessions."

The men of prayer tell us, therefore, that we must be "detached" from things. "Possess poverty," said St. Dominic; and it was his last will and testament to his followers. But how easy to misinterpret the idea of detachment! Some think it means that to avoid avarice we should persuade ourselves that things themselves are without value, a policy which appears in the fable in terms of sour grapes. What an insult to their Maker! And what a cowardly rejection of responsibility! It is our world, and we have to labor to restore it. There is no need to panic. Poverty of spirit is the opposite of avarice; avarice consists in a refusal to see and love things as things-in-themselves, and a determination to grab and possess and utilize them simply as means; poverty of spirit then, on the contrary, consists in a refusal to grab and possess and utilize things, and a determination to see and love them in themselves. It is only, after all, a question of learning to be a contemplative. Imagine saying, when you see the breath-taking swoop of birds on the wing, "I must have that!" You have seen it and it is already yours. "A thing of beauty is a joy for ever"—and it is of secondary importance whether or not you possess the title deeds.

But one wants to possess things, to have them always near at hand, precisely because one does see and love them as things in themselves? Yes, indeed; but you are not perfectly detached so long as you are selfishly possessive and would refuse to surrender them if justice or charity or your own integrity demanded it. The contemplative is not for ever mourning the passing of things, like Herrick and his daffodils; on the contrary—"Consider the lilies of the field, how they *grow*"—there is an unquenchable joy in the Christian saint underlying all the sorrow; for though the passing of loveliness is necessarily and sometimes unbearably sad, still in eternity the beauty for ever is, and when you think not of having but of being, you go beyond the transience of time, you are *become* the daffodil, the bird, the girl, and your one-ness with them cannot be taken from you. You are living *in* love; and though time and space can hurt you horribly, they cannot destroy your oneness, for that, in its essence, is inde-pendent of them. The avaricious man is immersed in the time process, dreading the losses the future may bring. The poor in spirit live in the present, because they live in the Presence. "I live, now not I but Christ," said St. Paul; and "I know that nothing shall separate me" from Him; and for the world, we know that "God saw all the things that he had made, and they were very good," and though in themselves they come to be and pass away, yet they are all for ever present to Him in the eternal "now," so that to the extent we can live in that present we too can see beyond the tragedy of transience.

What I have can be taken from me; but what I am abides. The tension between the two worlds remains: if the things I love and the persons I love are taken from me I am miserable, I may be heart-broken; but if I have learnt to be poor in spirit, to love and not to grab, then I know in my soul that having or not-having cannot alter being, and I shall not fall into despair. Having nothing I shall still—in the sense that matters most—possess all things. The statement is indeed accurate: there is no limit to the extent to which the detached of spirit can be enlarged; for seeing God in all things, they find all things lovely and are one with them, and being able to contemplate instead of grabbing, they are not restricted to their own or even to common property (provided only that other men's fences are not too high). But of the man who grabs and clings you find that the more he has the less in truth he is, his possessions enslave and diminish him: enslave because he cannot move unless his whole ponderous array of possessions goes with him, diminish because he is thus not his own master, he is dependent on the very things he has tried to make his own creatures. Things that are possessed without detachment of spirit tend to drain life more and more out of the possessor: but to be one with things in poverty of spirit is to have their own life added to one's own.

In the inner life of the mind also we have to learn poverty of spirit, to die in order to be reborn. The autonomous self attempts to make reason a supreme arbiter and the creator of truth; it wakes up to find itself a king with no court. If you regard things simply as means, the power of vision fades in you; trying to assume a greater power than you really have, you find you lose control even of the things that are, in fact, your servants: senses and instincts go their ways independent of you. So you must either acquiesce in disintegration or try to thrust the rebellious elements out of sight till they re-emerge from the underworld and destroy you. Here, too, some think that the way to restore the essential power of vision is to repudiate and destroy the other ways of knowledge and judgment. And again it would be no restoration at all. It is wholeness that we have to try to recover.

There are many ways in which the human person can reach out to reality; and they are all indispensable if he is to be whole. To suppose that science is all is silly; to suppose that reason is all is silly; to suppose that the senses are all is subhuman; but also to suppose that vision is all is, though in a different way, sub-human, for it is reversing instead of remedying the original disaster, and recovering the child only in order to liquidate the man. Some people are so dismayed by the vagaries of the human reason that they renounce it altogether, and think that a divine voice will guide them immediately at every turn. Reason was rightly called the candle of the Lord. To abandon it is an insult to Him; it is also a form of self-destruction. The saints, who submit their direct experience of God to a ruthless rational analysis lest they be deceiving themselves, and who at the same time use reason to investigate, judge, plan, decide, all the affairs moral and material that concern them in the world—they are the ones who are whole.

It is reason's right and office to control. But like the centurion it must both exercise and submit to authority: it cannot rule unless it also obeys, for its power is delegated. As long as we try to *make* truth to meet our requirements we go inevitably astray: it cannot be made; it can only be discovered. And it can be discovered only by the poor in spirit. The way to wisdom, as Augustine said, is firstly humility and secondly humility and thirdly humility. Was it not T. H. Huxley who said, "We must sit down before fact like a child"? That is the way to be a scientist. And to sit down before truth like a child is the way to be a philosopher, as the word itself—"*lover* of wisdom"—might tell us. If you try to bluster and browbeat truth, she will elude you; if you woo her with the humility of the lover, she will come to you.

At every level, therefore, the proud self must die if the personality is to be reborn. We need the ascesis of the mind as well as of the senses. So the men of prayer tell us that the way to union with God passes through the "dark night," both of sense and of soul; that when we set ourselves to open to God's touch the inner depths of the spirit, we must still, not only senses and imagination, but reason too. They must learn their place. Between disintegration and integrity there is the lesson of concentration to be learnt.

But in its own domain also reason must die. We are familiar enough in theory with the way in which the judgment of reason can be colored and, indeed, determined by unconscious prejudices and desires. It is hard to be objective; and the unmortified mind will be forever distorting the truth in the service of the pseudo-self. We degrade reason if we use its powers to "rationalize," as the psychologists say, what we really know to be wrong. Between dishonest rationalizations and objective reasoning there is the lesson of docility to be learnt. There are times when only through the good offices of others can we break through the mists of our own prejudices and come to the truth; but at all times we are finite and fallible, and in the waging of the cosmic war with evil, we desperately need the guiding revelation of God.

No need to stress the way in which the senses can cheat us. These ways of union with reality are observable in their truly natural state in the aesthetic experience, when in and through the senses the whole personality is possessed by beauty and is filled with joy, and in a different manner in some of the moments which love brings, when again it is in and through the senses that a whole union of persons is brought about and expressed. But this wholeness is not our common state. "Catch us the little foxes that destroy the vines": the senses have their own pursuits, and pull us this way and that in defiance of integrity, and spill and squander the deep, dark wine of life; and reason is persuaded to rationalize and excuse their vagaries, and the pseudo-self tries to believe it is happy… Here, too, we desperately need the revelation and the power of God.

We are involved in the cosmic struggle because we must fight either for one side or the other, there is no neutrality; but also because we are ourselves its battleground: "Simon, Simon, behold Satan hath desired to have you that he may sift you as wheat." The evidence points to the presence of an energy of evil greater than man in the world; the evidence points also to the presence of an energy of good greater than man in the world. This is the age-old dream of humanity: that humanity through dying the death, through making the long, dark sea-journey, through the slaying of the dragon, might be made whole by its return to the One who is All in all; and the Christian believes that the reality fulfils the dream. The energy of good in the world is the divine energy, and we can share it. It is the life and power of God that can inter-inanimate us; for Christ has died the sacrificial death and lain in the tomb and gone down into hell and risen, and in His might we can do the same. I can share the life of flower and bird and human being, and be one with them; but all that means nothing unless it is the real I and not the false one; and of myself I can do nothing—how can we expect the pseudo-self to dethrone itself? But we know something of how love can enable one personality to inspire, to breathe life into, another, and it gives us some dim insight into the way in which Christ can give us His life and His power. Evil can take possession of us; but God can take possession of us too.

Christ is still in the world today. The Catholic believes that the Church is the prolongation in time of the life of Christ; and that the whole of the sacramental system, and the Mass in particular, is the divine means of bringing this life and power to man, as the teaching authority of the Church is the divine means of guarding and interpreting the revelation of God, and so of guiding the reason of man. But God waits upon our will. There are some who argue that this doctrine of sacraments and divine life and power cannot be true for the simple reason that, if it were, the practicing Christians would necessarily be so different from the pagans, so immense a force for good in the world; and, in fact, they are not. "God is love," they quote at us, and then they add, "See how these Christians love one another!"

It is a strong argument. In the days when the Church was young and small and poor and persecuted, those words were a tribute, wrung unwillingly from the pagan world by the sight of the charity of Christians. They shared what little they had with one another; they loved and served each other even unto death; they knew no distinctions of caste or class or nation; they called themselves brothers and sisters and they meant what they said. Then in time the Christian religion became the established religion of the empire of Rome, wealthy, powerful, secure; men became Christians in name who were far from the spirit of Christ; and rival sects sprang up and rent the Body of Christ; and in the followers of the God of Love the pagans saw selfishness, envy, dissensions, enmity. And again they said, "See how these Christians love one another"; but this time they said it with a laugh.

The centuries went by, and the face of Europe changed; the independent nations were born, Christian in name, outwardly acknowledging the authority of Christ. Yet again and again these nations made war on one another, slaughtered one another, laid waste the lands, defied the Father of Christendom, and left behind them a legacy not of love but of hate. See how *these* Christians loved one another. Half a century ago, a great Pope spoke in words of fire of the hideous thing we call the class war, a war not against strangers but against neighbors, the sons of the same hearths. He was speaking primarily to Christians, yet his voice passed almost unheeded, and the scandal of injustice and enmity went on... The pagans still ask, "Where is this charity, where is this power, of which we hear so much?"

It is a strong argument, and God forgive us if we ever try to turn it with a debating reply. It has truth in it, though it is not the whole truth. If we look at the average group of respectable Christians, do we not feel obliged sometimes to say they are no better than their neighbors? Must we not say the same of ourselves (even though we know also in our hearts that, but for the power of Christ, we should be infinitely worse than we are)? But it is not the whole truth; and sometimes when the argument is weighing most heavily on one's consciousness, one comes suddenly upon a simple greatness of soul, a holiness, the mystery of a rare, deep, selfless love blazing into brilliance in an unlikely place, and one is brought to one's knees. It is difficult to miss the noisy scandals of wars and hatreds; it is easier to miss the small, quiet devotion and love and integrity of the millions of simple men and women through the ages who strengthen and sweeten the lives of those with whom they live.

But, in any case, God does not work by violence or magic; He waits upon the human will. I am no better but rather worse than my pagan neighbor: it proves, not that the life and power of God are not offered me, but that I for my part keep them away. What was done in and by Christ must be done again in and by the Christian; with Christ he must cross over the brook. When evil takes possession of man, it works in him by naked power and violence; but God takes posses-

sion by the power of love, precisely that we may learn that
the only real power *is* love.

Love waits upon the will of the beloved. Yet everything
short of violence it will do, when the beloved is in need. With
the pseudo-self enthroned, we are helpless to save ourselves;
and so God, through the Church's baptism, brings the baby
into divine life, or, through the promptings with which He
touches the heart, leads the adult to seek Him in the Church.
It is the constant theme of the baptismal rite: a liberation
from the power of evil and darkness, and so a birth into new
life. Three times the priest breathes in the face of the one to
be baptized and says, "Go out from him, unclean spirit, and
give place to the Holy Spirit, the Comforter." Again he
breathes on his face in the form of a cross, saying, "Receive
the good spirit by this inbreathing and the blessing of God.
Peace be with you." Later he commands again, "Hear, cursed
spirit of evil . . . and go forth. . . . Give honor to the approaching Holy Spirit, coming down from the highest heaven
to set your deceits at naught and to make of this heart,
cleansed in the divine font, a blessed temple and dwelling for
God." And once again: "Go forth, unclean spirit, and give
honor to God, the living and true. Begone, unclean spirit,
and give place to Jesus Christ, His Son. Depart, unclean
spirit, and give place to the Holy Spirit, the Comforter."

It is in the driving forth of world, flesh and devil that the
false autonomous self dies; in the coming of Father, Son and
Holy Spirit that the real self is reborn. Our Lord drove forth
the buyers and sellers from the Temple; the new self is to be
the temple of God, and the grasping, utilizing self must be
driven forth. The world in the Gospel sense is precisely this:
making the earth and all that is in it not the handiwork of
God to be loved and reverenced, but the creature of the self

to be treated only as a means. The flesh in the Gospel sense is precisely this: treating man or woman, not as the child of God to be loved and reverenced, but as the creature of self, the means to pleasure. And the devil is the sovereign whom, through world and flesh and consequent rivalry, enmity and hatred, the would-be autonomous self adores; whereas, as William Law tells us, if we seek for God in everything, we shall surely find Him, and then "we shall be happy with all the happiness of God." For the evil trinity is of its essence isolation and therefore misery; the divine Trinity is of its essence the happiness of a shared life.

By baptism, then, we are born into a new and divine life. But we are only at the beginning of the long process of integration. It still remains for us, like the sun, to "die daily": to learn by constant effort (and constant failure) how to respond to the life and power within us. To know the indwelling Presence, we must pass through the dark nights; to establish reason in its proper power to judge and its ability to control, we must teach ourselves to be humble and docile; to recall the will and the senses to their proper life as elements in a whole personality, we must laboriously train them. And all this is to say that we must learn to be poor in spirit.

But we must do all this not for our own sakes alone. We are given the divine life also that we may be able to help to heal the world. It is not only the man that is exorcized in the baptismal service: it is the *creatura salis*, the salt, as well. If you read the *Rituale*, you will see the innumerable things for which a blessing is given. If you study the liturgy of the Mass, you will see the same thing: bread and wine as the essential fruits of the earth; the building, furnishings, vestments, sculpture, painting, song, for all the arts; the symbolism of lion and eagle and lamb and fish for all the animal creation;

the believers themselves as standing for all humanity—it is the whole of creation which is thus brought to the altar to be freed from evil and to be blessed. There is a Buddhist prayer which is said turning to the four quarters of the earth and to zenith and nadir, "May all beings be happy." The Catholic liturgy makes the same prayer: as the Church prays for health both of soul and body, so it is not spirit alone that is to be sanctified by the breath of divine life, but matter also; but it is not merely in prayer that the Church is concerned for these things, it is in power. In the rite of exorcism the priest is bidden to *command* the unclean spirit; for when Christ sent forth His followers to preach and to heal, He gave them *power.*

The vastness of the cosmic struggle is the measure of our responsibility as members of the Church. The past is with us still, awaiting redemption, as we know if we study the unconscious mind. My desires and actions cannot be conceived as though *in vacuo*: they come largely from the life I have inherited, from my immediate forbears first, and then, behind them, from the whole history of the race and ultimately of the world; they are still in great part bound to evil, and it is for me to play my part in restoring them. The future waits and depends upon us now; for we, too, shall live in those who follow, an influence either for good or for ill. Even in the present we can never stand alone; we do not know the extent to which spiritual influences act and interact in defiance of distance, but there are indications that they do; and what I do now in this place may directly affect others in another continent, and certainly will affect them indirectly, since by what I do the total balance of power between good and evil is necessarily changed.

And as the human family is bound up in this way with my personal obedience to the energy of good in the world, so

the rest of creation also. The whole of creation is in travail...
We cannot hope to restore the whole of our lost dominion;
we cannot hope that the divine order will be fully restored.
But there is much that we can do—provided that we have
learnt that true dominion is the dominion of love. You do not
restore the right relationship by keeping wild animals in
prison behind bars. Those who originally domesticated our
dogs and cats and horses were wiser and more reverent than
we. Mme. David-Neel on one of her journeys woke up to
find a leopard sniffing near her: "'Little thing,' I murmured,
looking at the graceful animal, 'I have seen, near to, a much
bigger prince of the jungle than you. Go to sleep and be
happy.' I doubt whether the 'little thing' understood me.
However, after a few minutes it went leisurely away."[2] "May
all beings be happy"—but they depend upon us.

In all these things—the recovery of our own integrity, the
recovery of the human family, the restoration of the happiness of the world of nature as well as of men—we are
brought back to the recognition of the presence of evil, the
sense of sin. Without that we may go on skimming placidly
along the surface of life and thinking that all is well with us.
We are given the gift of pain because it can lead us to fear and
reverence and then to love; and when we have become truly
lovers, we can become masters again because we shall say, "I
can do all things" only "in Him who strengtheneth me."

Yesterday I saw a girl torn by a passing lorry that had suddenly mounted the pavement. Her leg had been ripped right
open along its length, and, as she lay, the foot quivered and
twitched spasmodically like a small, hurt animal. Had she
sinned, or her parents. . . ? Our Lord on another occasion

---

[2] Alexandra David-Neel: *My Journey to Lhasa,* Penguin ed., 39.

answered, "Neither, but that the works of God might be made manifest."

People sometimes say that the answer to the problem of pain which rests upon its power to make us live breaks down in so far as it is not only the ones who need pain (and still less have deserved it) to whom it comes. Perhaps there are very few of whom it might be said that they do not need pain, though indeed there are some whose childlike loveliness and wisdom you feel can stand in no need of pain's tutelage. But I do not know that that is the essential point. There are some who suffer too early: can pain bring wisdom to the undeveloped mind of the child? (Unless, indeed, it can be transmuted later, when the mind can catch up, and see into the past experience.) There are some whom presumably pain can never teach but only torment—the animals. But the animal and the child and the girl also are not alone, they are not just individuals; we are all a family. A mother does not resent suffering for her child; the agony is, on the contrary, when she cannot suffer instead of her child; and we know that mystery of sympathy whereby, in fact, it is impossible for the child to suffer without the mother's suffering too. That sharing of consciousness should not be confined to the inner life of the home; we are all a family.

If only we had that insight about each other and about the world of nature, we should not be so hopelessly puzzled by pain. It would not cease to be a problem; we never get to the end of the mystery of sin. But, at least, we should be more readily consoled. The torn girl lay like a shattered thing on the pavement, a stolid crowd stood and gazed, a woman shuddered with pleasure because she had had a thrill; but even if the thing did not jolt a single soul in the crowd from acceptance of surface existence to a recognition, however dim, of the deeper things, even if it did not so much as sow a seed in a single mind which would bear fruit later in other circumstances, still it was a part of a greater thing, it was a part of the travail of the whole creation, and wherever the mystery of that travail strikes and rouses the mind of man, there it will be.

We suffer for one another even though we do it unconsciously; we suffer for one another that the spectacle of suffering may lead us to the dark journey, that the false self may die, that having now not the knowledge of good and evil that was sought in the primal sin, but the experience of the power and depths of evil and the power and glory of good, we may search for and find and drink of the fountain that springs up into life eternal, and, knowing at last the extent to which we are torn and wounded, may in the end be made whole.

III

The Vision of Man[1]

Nowhere is the degradation of the grasping, utilizing attitude to created things more terrible nor the loneliness that follows from it more profound than in the relationship between human beings. We are roused to fury when we see a barbarian destroying or insulting a work of art, still more if he ill-treats an animal; infinitely more if he ill-treats a child. Yet we seem to find it hard to see the same brutality in its less dramatic forms. We recognize the brutality of cruelty and we recognize the brutality which is blind to beauty; we do not always recognize the brutality of treating ends as means. We can see that the industrial magnate who treats his "hands" as though they were cattle is a disgrace to humanity; we do not always see so readily that to treat them as "hands" at all is a disgrace to humanity. We know that to ravish a woman is the act of a brute; but do we ever stop to wonder just how much that passes for love-making is also the act of a brute?

In both cases the sin is in essence the same. Begin by asking what a human being is. You will be led to answer first of all in terms of a sort of infinity. We have learnt much in recent

---

[1] In writing Chs. III and VI I have adapted and incorporated some material from a paper on Christian sex morality read to the Oxford University Socratic Club in November 1942, and (by kind permission of the Editor) from an article on the Sacrament of Marriage published in *Blackfriars,* May 1942.

years of the way in which the individual recapitulates the history of the race and of the world: not an isolated atom with nothing but his own personal history, but a storehouse of the age-old thoughts and desires and experiences of created things. Then there is the infinity of the mind's power to know, its power to "become in a manner all things." Above all, there is the divine destiny: to become one, not with all things merely, but with the Maker of all things. Secondly, you will be led to the quality of uniqueness. No two human beings are exactly alike; each is this particular body-spirit and not another, each has his own particular gifts and powers and qualities, his own heredity, his own partly inherited, partly determined, partly self-determined character and temperament, his own particular experience and way of reacting to experience. Because unique, he cannot without violence and degradation be regimented or dragooned; because infinite, he cannot be regarded simply as part of the finite world, still less of a finite social system, still less again of an economic structure. He is these things, indeed, as we shall see; but he is much more. In his infinity he overtops the world. It was the opinion of St. Thomas that the secrets of men's hearts are not part of the universe; not even the angels can know them: they stand in a direct relationship to God alone.

In the Middle Ages they had a maxim, *corruptio optimi pessima,* the greater the thing the deeper the degradation if it is corrupted. To treat men as economic "hands" or as political "units" in defiance of their uniqueness and infinity is a unique and infinite degradation: you are treating the greatest thing in the world as a means. To treat a human being as a means to pleasure and to call it love is the greatest degradation of all.

There are some people (the scientifically minded) who will not have the activities of hormones romanticized: for them, falling in love is just a biochemical reaction to appropriate stimuli, and should be treated with scientific freedom and detachment. Then there is the joyous pagan: he does, in a sense, love and worship beauty, but he interprets worship in a somewhat activist sense, and beauty in terms of consumption rather than production; he believes in gathering rosebuds, and though he weep as they droop and wither, he makes no attempt to stop the rot; like Herrick, he

> co'd never love indeed;
> Never see mine own heart bleed:
> Never crucifie my life
> Or for Widow, Maid, or Wife—

so that they for their part

> By and by
> ...do lie
> Poor girls, neglected.

These two types both forget that man lives a many-levelled life, but that it is the *man* who lives it. We are not just body, we are not just mind; we are not just body *and* mind either; we are body-mind. You cannot, once within the sphere of conscious activity, say that this or that affects the body but not the mind, the mind but not the body: everything that is done or experienced is done or experienced by the body-mind.

And, therefore, there is an essential difference between sex in man and sex in animals. Sex in man is all that the biologist says it is; but it is infinitely more, and more precious, than that. For in the union of two bodies, it is the union of two persons that can be achieved. That is why sex is a mystery: not a sinister or murky mystery, indeed, but a mystery. If you view sex simply as a biological function or a physical plaything you miss its whole meaning, and the deep human realities it could disclose to you will remain hidden. Nothing could be more inaccurate than to speak of Casanova as one of the world's great lovers: there can have been few men who knew less of love than Casanova, for he never, as far as one can see, touched reality at all, never emerged from the narrow, brittle shell of his own little ego.

But to be a Casanova is something worse than being only half a man: it is to treat other human beings as less than human too. The only possible human way in which we can approach human beings is with awe and reverence as towards a mystery, though admittedly the mystery is not without its humor. If we forget the mystery, we are brutish, even though we may not be brutal. It may be the blind animal brutishness that has never known the spirit, or it may be the shallow commercialized brutishness that exploits the body and ignores the mind; in either case it is a destruction of humanity because it cannot adore, it can only grab. We hate the tripper who cannot even contemplate a bluebell but has to tear and maul and destroy it; but how much worse to be unable to contemplate the human being, and to maul and destroy that!

Why is it that our world has exchanged art in its daily life for ugliness if not because it has lost its reverence for things? And why do we find ourselves condemned to live in a world that has exchanged love for hatred and enmity and rivalry if not because it has lost its reverence for men and women? There is a degradation worse than the carnage of the battle-field and the bombed city: you find it in the commercial exploitation which uses men as featureless economic units, you find it in the concentration camps which treat them as specimens for the sadist, and you find it in the private exploitation which treats them as pleasure-machines.

The soul of love-making is humility. Indeed, you must have a double reverence and humility; first, because there is no art without reverence, and love-making is an art in the simple sense of making what is true and good and beautiful; and secondly, because its material is not stone or paint, nor merely flesh, but the mysterious infinity of the person. Those teachers are very wise who tell us that humility is the ground of all the virtues; we are in evil case if we forget it, for it will mean that the false self and not the true is enthroned. We shall want to possess and domineer over truth and turn it to our own purposes instead of wanting it to take possession of us; and so we shall lose wisdom and prudence which are the humility of the mind. We shall want to domineer over things and be absolute owners and masters and treat them as mere utilities instead of remembering that we are only God's stewards and that things are to be loved and reverenced because they are the work of His hands; and so we shall not have poverty of spirit and we shall not have justice, for to have these is to be humble (in theory and in practice) about our possessions. We shall turn our aggressive instinct, our desire for mastery and power, to self-assertion and selfishness instead of harnessing our energies to the service of the Light; and so we shall lose fortitude, which is humility in strength and courage. And finally, we shall want to grab and domineer over bodily beauty and be arbitrary masters of our own bodily powers instead of accepting on our knees the gift of wholeness which love brings us; and so we shall lose temperateness, the humility of the flesh.

Temperateness is not the denial of passion; on the contrary:

Shall I compare thee to a summer's day?
Thou art more lovely and more temperate.

55

Spring is more temperate than summer; it is also more passionate. Temperateness is not the absence of passion, it is the transfiguring of passion into wholeness. Without it, you will have the chaos that follows the primal sin: you will have the senses usurping sovereignty and excluding the spirit; you will have them deciding good and evil and excluding God; you will have the destruction of the integrity of the person where you should have an immense enhancement of life. But is not temperateness always trying to tell us what not to do, trying to exclude and deny? No, it excludes only as a sculptor or an etcher excludes, in order to create form; it denies only in order to affirm. It is positive as the temperateness of spring is positive; but it is positive also as art is positive. Look at its opposite, the grasping mauling autonomy of dehumanized passion, if you want to see what it means to destroy.

We can learn a lesson from one of the great love-stories of our European heritage. Abelard wrote a treatise on the meaning of love, and much that was in it he owed to Cicero; but he owed more to Héloïse and to the wisdom with which she interpreted their tragedy. "It was desire more than love, *amicitia*, that bound you to me," she wrote to him; but of herself she said, "*Nihil unquam in te nisi te exquisivi*: Never did I seek anything in you save you yourself: you alone I wanted, not what you could give me." What the true lover loves is the beloved person, not just his own pleasure in her. He may ask gifts indeed; but the gifts on both sides are equally a receiving. He that loseth his life shall find it. The false self speaks of love, but it is a false love which is only a form of grabbing; there is no escape from the loneliness of the ego there. In real love we can hardly distinguish giving from getting: each is indistinguishably both. The lover's giving *is* his getting: that his gift should be lovingly accepted is itself a gift to him, and the gift he values most.

From reverence and humility we come to the understanding of love. With reverence we are already far from vulgarity and violence; with humility we leave behind us the shallows of selfish pleasure-seeking; it is with the love that comes of them that we shall find we have enlarged our life and immeasurably enriched it because in poverty of spirit we shall at last have enlarged our hearts. "With my body I thee *worship*," we say in the liturgy of marriage; without worship there is disaster as well as sin. At the height of passion especially it is easy to forget the person, to forget the breadth and depth of love, to let the hard-won unity of the self be split up again into fragments, and passion in autonomy become a preying brute. It is only by a habitual reverence and humility and worship that the danger can be forestalled. And always love-making demands patience and gentleness and sometimes heroic generosity if there is not to be the proud snatching of a selfish pleasure where there should be the deep oneness of a shared joy. Sexual pleasure is not a king in its own right; it is one element in a whole, and being one element only, it may not rule. It is one element in the totality of the oneness of two *persons*; if it is not that, if it is a dictator, it ceases to be human at all.

There is something very attractive about the joyous pagan gathering his rosebuds; but it is because we allow ourselves to forget the wholeness of the human situation and fix our attention on one element within it. Do you find it hard to *feel* that this is so? Think of the immensity of the total love of two human beings. At the height of passion, love produces ecstasy. The word means being outside the self: it means "I live, now not I," it means "It is thyself." A man and a woman are each unique and infinite: "I have said, Ye are gods." Here you have two infinities that are one: not a drab assuagement of tumescence, not a slick exercise of a biological function, not the feckless gathering of rosebuds, but the marriage of gods. Ecstasy means living in another. Here, you are living in the being you love; you are living in the race whose history you summarize, whose function you fulfil, whose life you gather in your hands and pass on to the future ages; you are living (if you have eyes to see) in God, to whose life and love you thus do homage, whose infinite mighty art waits upon you to work with you—you making the body, He the spirit—to fashion another infinity. This is the immensity that sex can open out to you; and will you isolate it and turn it into a toy? For here if anywhere it must be clear that you are not the master of heaven and earth, and that you must go down on your knees to receive a gift greater than yourself. It is the snatcher and the mauler who destroy; the temperate man adores.

You cannot grab at the infinite; you can only wait and worship. Christian temperateness is a form of worship first of all because every act of virtue is also, and primarily, an act of religion, but also in a special sense because its main purpose is to humble the senses and make ecstasy possible. It begins with a sort of loving fear: modesty in the modern sense and a kind of shyness and a sense of awe, and at the same time a fear of the ugliness of violence and of the power of passion to destroy integrity. And therefore, as complement to this initial reverence, there is the love of beauty, which is clarity and integrity; the spirit of nobility, of *gentilezza,* as opposed to the vulgarity of a personality in disintegration. Read the treatise of St. Thomas on temperateness in the *Summa Theologica* and you will find these two ideas constantly recurring; you will find some modes of virtue mentioned which do not immediately refer to physical love but which, nevertheless, because they go to make up the whole picture of the temperate man, help to make up the whole picture of the lover. You will find chastity described precisely as guarding the integrity of the body-spirit against disintegration; then you will find gentleness, which is an element in the worship of the lovely and the sacred; you will find clemency, which is opposed to cruelty, and, therefore, to the cruelty of using a human being as a means to pleasure. There is a vice of *curiositas*, which is not healthy curiosity but a desire for knowledge or experience which for one reason or another is disordered and destructive—and in this case would describe the dilettante who flits from one human being to another in search of novelty and so destroys the integrity of each, and always misses the deeps of reality. There is *modestia*, which guards against the violation of that privacy and intimacy of the body-spirit to which love alone can give access, and then ensures that love-play shall not be robbed of its integrity by being turned into an experiment in selfish localized pleasure instead of the sharing of a deep personal joy.

And then you find a discussion of humility and the primal sin of pride. It is the root of the whole matter. The other virtues, too, are grounded in humility and destroyed by pride; but the death of the false self day by day, the challenging of the false self where its brutality and the effects of its arrogance can be most marked, is especially the task of temperateness. You will find, too, a discussion of death as the wages of sin, of this primal sin; and of the servility of intemperance because especially it is destructive of beauty. The chaste man is free, not because he is passionless, but because his passion does not destroy but expresses and enlarges the spirit; and chastity brings not death but life because, just as in the aesthetic vision it is in and through the senses that the whole being is enlarged, so here too, and to an infinitely deeper and wider extent, it is in and through the senses that the two infinities meet and are made one.

Corruptio optimi pessima. You have to be so careful when you hold in your hands a thing of great loveliness and value. Think how tenderly we treat a glass of wine of rare vintage, and rightly; yet that is not infinite, that is not a person, that cannot be hurt as a man or a woman can be hurt. You can hurt love and yourself and the other, if you wrench the physical from its human totality; or if you are selfish and use the other as a means; or if you are proud in the primal sense of denying the mystery and excluding God. Christian temperateness is not the tempered possessive enjoyment of things, but rather a worshipping union *with* things *in* God; it is saying to another human being, "It is thyself," so that both together in their oneness may make the final affirmation to the Infinite Love, "It is Thyself."

This gentleness is not just an external thing. It is not primarily an external thing. It is primarily a gentleness of mind. How terrible when people are led to believe, or left to believe, that once they are in love they have nothing to do but live happy ever after, they have nothing further to learn. Love is an endless creative process; the oneness of the two is not born but made.[2] Do you think that two people, however much in love, will love each other in exactly the same way? Do you think they will never differ in the way they want to express their love? Do you think that because they are living in love they cease to be individuals, or that the false self is

[2] Cf. Chapter VI.

wholly dead? There is always the tension; there is always the temptation to sink back into the separate selfhood, there is always the danger that passion may destroy the unity of the person; it is only by long, patient labor that you can hope to forge the unity of the deep personal will which can govern separate superficial desire.

So, when you make love you must be gentle and humble, because it is to the mystery of a human being that you are making love. Love is an endless creative process; it is also an endless voyage of discovery. Because you are in love with each other do you think you know each other? Perhaps when you are both old you will have learnt a little—but only if all the time you have loved deeply and been deeply aware of your ignorance. And if you are proud and refuse to accept your ignorance, if you are proud and try to dictate to this shared life which is so much greater than your own, then you will kill your real self though no doubt you will not notice it, and you will kill the heart it should have been your glory to serve. If you accept your ignorance and know your smallness in face of this mystery, then you will make many mistakes, you will find your passion imperfect because of its ability to make you forget love, you will know pain and disappointment and repentance, but you will be able to be reborn and be a child. Here especially the grain of wheat must fall into the ground lest itself remain alone.

If you degrade love by brutality or selfishness or pride, you destroy it; and you will find its wholeness broken up into two fragments, each of them ugly; you will find passion twisted into lust, and emotion twisted into sentimentality. Both of them are superficial, both of them are unreal, both of them are disruptive; and their fruit is loneliness. When passion breaks away from the deep life of a man it can never enlarge him, it has nothing to say to the heart; it can never be a marriage of gods, only an animal mauling its prey. When emotion breaks away from the deep will of a man it runs away from reality; it makes for itself a fantasy-object which obscures the real; endlessly agitated over the superficial well-being of its object it never goes down to the depths to find the real good and the real evil; there is no meeting, it can never help.

We live a many-levelled life, and real love is a sharing of life on all these levels, but a sharing of them in their integrity, a sharing of the whole being; and that is why the fullness of love is not likely to be given us this side the grave for we are not likely this side the grave to be completely whole. But though the fullness of love is something that must wait upon our wholeness, love itself is precisely what makes us whole; when we have the fullness we say, "It is thyself," but it is love that makes us begin to say it.

Lust and sentimentality separate, but love unites; and God who is Love Redemptive gives us love with its joys and sorrows to restore our wholeness, to bring us in again out of the cold. He gives us love with its joys and especially its sorrows because it can lead us to rebirth. If you skim along the surface of life, you will never know the need of a Savior except by hearsay, for you will never know the depths of the human heart. If love were an endless idyll unflecked by sorrow you would be endlessly happy, but you would not know the intensity of happiness as you might, for you would still not know the depths of the human heart. But if you know the love that can lead you near to heartbreak, if you know not only the heights of ecstasy but the depths of pain, then you will know you stand before a mystery and you will be silenced, you will have seen the abyss of the human heart which only infinity can fill, and perhaps you will find yourself forced to look beyond the barriers of the finite for the Love in which all other loves are fulfilled.

To say "I love you in God" may be an insult; but not if we say it aright. Created things live only by and in the Uncreated; to see them apart from Him is to see them out of their true element. It is not seeing them in God that does violence to them or diminishes their reality, it is seeing them apart from Him; for just as passion is destroyed when it ceases to live in the wholeness of the person, so things are destroyed when they are abstracted from the eternal Whole. To see and love in God is not to see and love a shadow; it is to see and love the real where it is most real. The daffodils haste away and are lost to us; but they are forever present in the eternal "now." If you love the daffodil in the isolation of idolatry, your love dies when it fades and is gone; if you love it in the Eternal, you love it forever. And the human being? You do not love aright unless you love in humility and worship; and will you be more humble and reverent or less when you know that the being you love and God are one? Will you be more gentle or less, more afraid of selfish domineering and violence or less? With all your strength you will be temperate, for you will know that your hands hold the temple of God.

You want to be master and maker, and you are right; but you cannot be these things unless you have learnt to love, and to love as we ought is hard. So God, whose love makes things lovely, gives you this particular human love to make things easier for you. If you want to see what real tenderness is, look at the love of God: you will not find in Him any sentimentality, you will find no weak humanitarian mildness in the infinite consuming Fire, no shielding us from the Pain that can show us what life means; but you will find tender-

63

ness that tempers the winds for the shorn lamb, that will do anything, short of violence to its own gift of free will, to lead us back in spite of ourselves to wholeness, that will run the risk of defeat by a finite rival rather than leave us without this best and greatest signpost to itself. God is Lover and Maker; He made us in His image, to know Him and love Him and serve Him and be happy; and we serve Him by being lovers and makers in our turn, but lovers first and then makers, for His creation is the expression of His love. He made us to know and love Him and to be makers: it is the same journey that leads us to both ends: to find the vision of the One and to be makers we must learn to love, and to love we must learn to accept the gift of pain.

You want to be master and maker; but for that you must learn the reality of love and not its romanticized shadow. You can, if you like, close your eyes to the pain and toil and tension that love involves and build instead a fantasy world from which difficulties and conflicts are excluded and the days pass by in a haze of cloudless happiness and it is always spring; but the wages of this sin is death. The sort of making which does not spring from worship is brutality; but the sort of making which does not spring from the worship of reality is a sham. If you romanticize the harshness of reality, you hitch your wagon to a tinsel star; you may deceive yourself all your life long, you may find pleasure which will pass muster as happiness; but sooner or later reality will obtrude itself, and the whole fabric will dissolve, and perhaps it will be too late then to build again with solid bricks and stones. We are not children in a feckless limbo but men and women in a world of travail, where loveliness is flecked with sorrow, and ecstasy is often begotten of pain; and we can be lovers and makers only when our hearts have been battered and broken on reality, and so have learnt to make their whole life a whisper of worship like the murmur of the sea.

Love, like prayer, has its moments of ecstasy; but it is made up not of these but of the simplicities, the common joys and burdens, of every day. It is a long and laborious process, though its drudgeries are suffused with joy. We are led to it because of our incompleteness, because the heart is a hunger, because we are always seeking for fulfilment of body, mind and will. Man and woman complete one another, but the demands of passion will not always coincide: there is the labor and sometimes the agony of approaching, touching, entering, another mind, there is a long labor of forging the unity of the deep personal will. We live in a world where the realities of love are often obscured, for love itself is largely disintegrated into lust and sentiment. In a world that is grasping, greedy, self-seeking, the reality of worship needs to be explained to us. In a world that speaks of love as a romanticized passion, we need to be shown the labor it involves.

The young especially need to be told that love is not a glamorous fairy tale, but a life-work which involves all the patient toil that no great life-work, no great art, can avoid. But they need to be told, too, that it is a divine destiny, which the life of God within us can make both easier and more glorious.

They need to be told that in order to open their eyes and hearts, God may lead them near to heartbreak; but they need to be told, too, of the deep abiding happiness and the moments of dazzling glory, of the joys that will come to them, not in the next world only when their troubles are over, but in this world too.

They need to be told of the greatness of the love of man and woman as ministers of God's omnipotence, as makers with God of what will not pass away. They need to be told to expect failures and misunderstandings, for the perfect work is not made in a day; but they need to be told, too, that the failures need never be final but, on the contrary, like every evil, can be made the material of a deeper awareness and a more perfect love.

They need to be told that there may be times when they will cry their eyes out with fright or with sorrow; but they need to be told, too, that there will be times when they will cry their eyes out for joy. They need to be told not to be afraid of idolatry or of God's rivalry provided they love Him faithfully; for their love is His will and their worship of Him, and is only deepened and strengthened by their prayer if they pray, as they should, hand in hand.

You want to be a maker, and you cannot make unless you have learnt to love; but if you are a lover, then indeed you are inescapably a maker, for loving is itself making. By their love the two are made one; the long, laborious process is itself happiness because it is the making of life: the daily sharing of joys and burdens, of work and play, of deepening vision and of worship—all this is love-making, and the making of love is the making of life. But love is endlessly self-diffusive: the two are made one most completely in and through their common making of the family; and the family in its turn, if it is living in love, will not rest in a private, enclosed beatitude, but will shed its light and warmth in an ever-widening arc of love and service upon the world.

The love of humanity can be romanticized as the love of man and woman can be romanticized: it is possible to feel sentimentally devoted to humanity and to hate and despise men and women. But the family that is living in love will be one of those lovely homes where the doors seem always to be open and the rooms always full—full of all sorts of oddities as well as all sorts of loveliness, full of the waifs and strays of society as well as the immediate circle of friends, full because you find there at all times the unassuming glory of charity, which is love and reverence for every human being and the warmth and welcome of home.

It is with our love as with our material possessions and all our gifts: we are only stewards. The love that is given us is meant to serve others besides ourselves; it is meant to lead us to the labor of helping to heal humanity and the stricken world. Here, above all, it is a terrible thing to bury our talent in a napkin. It is Love that mediates and makes at-one-ment between God and men. If you are given the gift of love, it is not least in order that you, too, may mediate. Love is power; to love in God is to love in the power of God and to act with the power of God; if you are faithful to the love and the power, you will mediate because you will bear God's blessing and holiness to the world and so help to restore it to Him: you will help to bring back creation to its fullness in the life of man, and the life of man and the world together to its fullness in the infinity of the life of God.

But the wicket swings "between the Unseen and Seen." Human love can be doubly our teacher: it can lead us to the threshold of God's throne, and then returning filled with His life it can illuminate the world for us, teach us to love the whole of God's handiwork and so to heal and strengthen and console. But the wicket swings; there is an imperiousness and a power to absorb us in this love of another human being which may lead us to refuse the double lesson. We may want to say, "This is all, and everything else a distraction"; or we may want to say, "Later I will worship, but not now." There were some in the Gospel parable who would not come to the banquet because of their business concerns—they were the men of power, condemned to remain alone. But there was another who had married a wife...

This is the greatest tragedy: when two who are one, who have been reborn in one another, who have, therefore, gone infinitely beyond the empty unreality of the man who remains alone, and stand as it were at the gates of paradise, nevertheless turn away—because they, too, have great possessions. This is the greatest tragedy: that you can repeat in company with another the lonely disintegration of the primal sin; that even though you are living in love you can turn away from Love. And then the original disruption is repeated: just as pride tears man from God and robs his nature of its wholeness, so this pride, too, tears love from its eternity and robs it even of its temporary wholeness.

Is this last untrue? Because the wicket shuts against the Infinite must love become intemperate? No, it can be temperate, it can worship, it can be irreproachable—but can it be these things except at the expense of something else? In one of two ways I think it must fail of perfect wholeness. It can be temperate at the expense of depth, it can be temperate because the horizon is foreshortened, the mystery reduced to clear and distinct proportions with which reason can be competent to deal; perhaps we are back in the eighteenth century? Or, like the great Romantics, it can cling to the depth and the mystery; it can cling to the immensity of living in love; and then, though like them it will have its liturgy of worship, I wonder whether the forces it unleashes will not be sometimes beyond its control. Apollo or Dionysus: it must invoke the one or the other; yet we can follow neither alone if we want reality, for each is only a fragment of the whole.

The love of the one we love can lead us to the love of the One, though our way is surer if we have first seen Him and learnt to live in eternity and then are given His gift of human love. It remains to turn, or to turn again, to the many; and the love of God gives us the power, the love of man gives us experience of the pattern; we should not now treat things as means. How can you help thinking when you see a society in which human beings are treated as "hands" or political units that it must be a society which has forgotten how to love? How can you help thinking when you see a society in which there is much lust and a welter of sentiment that it must be a society which has destroyed love? And if so, then why bother to make blueprints for a world society—the first thing is to rebuild the home. We are all a family. You cannot build a world society by reason alone; imagine a home which was run by reason alone—it would be not a home but a hell. We shall not be rid of injustice and hatred and war until we have learnt how to love. It is so obvious that it seems a platitude; but we forget that to love is to say, "It is thyself"; to love is to reverence and worship, to be temperate and tender.

But am I really expected to love every one and everything like this? Am I really expected to reverence and worship the washerwoman, the dustman, the man who brings the milk? Yes, you are; and the mongrel dog and the stray cat, too. But you are expected to love them, not to be sentimental. If you have seen worship interpreted in terms of simpering statues with little lace frills, if you have seen brotherhood interpreted in terms of oily smirks and the sort of conversation that is kind to be cruel, if you have seen temperateness interpreted in terms of a mealy-mouthed horror at the joys and realities of life, then, indeed, you might well recoil.

But only look at the opposite of worship and reverence,

look at the opposite of the temperate and the tender. You have seen a thing in these days whereby the whole world is degraded and the whole race of man; you have seen two million Jews torn from their homes, transported, massacred. No need to idealize them, no need to romanticize; some of them no doubt were great and noble, many were charming, but many also were no doubt unattractive and perhaps repulsive, the sort of man or woman you might avoid in the street. But they were human beings. They were human beings, each unique and with a sort of infinity about them, each capable of sharing the life of God.

And now look at your own life and your own surroundings. You may have authority over many, you may be in an exalted position, you may be counted among the great, and there is no need to sentimentalize and so embarrass other people. But if ever you use your authority to treat men as featureless units, your position to look through people as though they were not there, if ever your greatness induces you to think of the failures as beneath contempt, then you are doing to them what was done to these Jews. There is a difference of degree, not of kind.

If you treat men as units, you treat them as cattle. Humility is not maudlin; it is only truth. Our Lord did not hesitate to call evil men (and they were evil because they were proud) a brood of vipers; the saints have not been accustomed to mince their words; but beneath the evil there is still the uniqueness and the infinity, and it is *this*, you find, that the saints will never forget. We take our sides in the struggle of good with evil; but if we fight for good, we labor to love and to heal. Even where there is obvious wickedness, we must protest and fight against the external crime, indeed, but we may never judge of sin because we can never know the

70

human heart. There was one woman who was thought wicked, and men were preparing to stone her; but our Lord who did know the heart sent her away in peace. Perhaps she is now high in glory.

Our task is to love and to heal and so to follow remotely in His footsteps. But you cannot love without reverence; you cannot heal unless you are tender—for it is loneliness that we have to heal.

And the dog and the cat? They too are our responsibility. In Rome, there is a little forum which used to be a sort of home for stray cats; the pomp and tinsel efficiency of Fascism have long since swept them away. On the other hand, there are some who would pass unmoved by a starving beggar, but are white with fury if they see an animal insufficiently cared for. Temperateness gives us, among other things, proportion: sentimentality becomes most outrageous when passion, which should be fulfilled in the love of human beings, is driven underground and repressed. We must put things in their right order.

In the beginning, God planted a garden. We cannot return to it, but we can do something to recover what was lost. We come from the Good, who is our home; but we come into evil, for "there hath passed away a glory from the earth"; we have to try with toil and tears to make our way back, and the way back is the way of love and worship. All our life is meant to be that: the love and worship of the one we love and the many we love and the earth we love, within the love and worship of the God who is Love. And if we try to keep to that way, we shall do more than receive the healing power of God into ourselves: we shall walk not alone but together with these others we love, helped and helping; and as we come gradually nearer to God, our love will deepen and widen and grow stronger, we shall share more and more in Christ's healing love and power, and so, because our lives in themselves will be an affirmation of the reality to be restored, we shall be among the company of those who lead humanity and the whole earth back, a family, to its home.

IV

The Vision of the Way

The way back to God is the way of worship. If all that we are and become and do in our many-levelled life could be made one in worship, we should be saints. Some people think that Christian morality is no more than a series of Don'ts; others a little less ill-informed think it is no more than a series of Do's. These things are included, for being and doing are interdependent; but it is being that comes first in importance; and Christian morality tells us first of all not what we should do, still less what we should not do, but what we should be.

That is why you cannot possibly separate, as some people would have us do, the Church's moral teaching from its beliefs about God's revelation of Himself to the world. You cannot possibly separate them, because the moral teaching is entirely determined by the doctrine; and if you try to isolate it, you destroy it. You could isolate this or that element in it; you could cling to the ideals of justice, kindness, generosity, fortitude; but these virtues would then cease to be the Christian virtues, because they would be divorced from worship.

You find a marked similarity on the surface between the *Ethics* of Aristotle and that part of the *Summa* of St. Thomas which deals with morality; but the similarity is far less striking than the difference. Aristotle will tell you how to act wisely and well in accordance with reason, and what he says is often so true and so salutary that St. Thomas is at pains to repeat it; but all that is secondary, all that is relatively unimportant; you can obey all these precepts and acquire all these good habits and still find at the end that the "good life" has been led by the false self and not by the true. These things are secondary; what is of first importance is the reality whose presence kindles and whose absence kills them: the rebirth of the self in God, the recognition that God and not the ego is the centre of the self.

You remember the Pharisee and the Publican in the Temple. The Pharisee was living the "good life"; but notice what he says: "I give thanks . . . I fast . . . I give tithes," and the good deeds turn to ashes because it is always "I"; it is the self which competently acts, the self which is served; there is no suggestion of need of the Other, the hunger of the heart is forgotten because pride has repressed it. The Publican probably fails miserably to live the "good life," but he has the core of Christian as opposed to pagan morality, he has the one thing necessary, the pearl of great price, because he has learnt that he must say with his whole being not "I" but "Lord."

Christian morality is worship. There are prohibitions: they are the minimum, though many of us find that even this minimum is more than we can achieve. Thou shalt not kill, thou shalt not steal, thou shalt not commit adultery, thou shalt not covet: it is not always easy to keep these and all the lesser prohibitions of anger and injustice and intemperateness which they include. But notice how Christianity changes them. Thou shalt love: this is the essence of Christian morality; and to love is to dethrone the false self and be able to say, "It is thou." You are forbidden, then, to kill and steal and covet; but you are forbidden *because* these are sins against love, because they hurt those with whom you should be living in love. The proud man may refrain from these things because it is to his own interest; the Christian must refrain from these things primarily because if he does not he cannot love, he cannot live life in its wholeness, he cannot worship.

But a second thing follows. If it is love that leads you to refrain from injustice, it will lead you to more than that. As love grows deeper and wider in you and you come nearer to the fullness of life, you will find that this minimum becomes hopelessly insufficient; you will find the negative carried further and further over to the affirmation of its opposite. The saint's love prompts him not to kill in the service of the false self, but to sacrifice his own life if need be in the service of God and men; not to steal for himself, but to share all that he has with others; not to destroy a family life by wrecking its unity, but to give himself, even perhaps by forgoing his own family life, to restoring the family life of the world. Whatever he does is done thus as worship of the One and of the many in the One. How terrible when we find ourselves thinking of the moral law as a denial of freedom and happiness. These things are not wrong because they are forbidden: they are forbidden because they are wrong; and they are wrong because they are alien to the nature of man in general—because freedom and a full and dignified human life are impossible until they are outlawed; but principally because they make it impossible to escape from isolation, they make it impossible for us to love.

The lover does not find that love takes his freedom from him; on the contrary, he is tied and unhappy only if he is impeded from serving what he loves. If we obey the commandments because we fear that otherwise we shall be punished, we are not yet emancipated from the "bondage of the law" of which St. Paul speaks, we are not yet free. If we keep the commandments because we recognize that they are the necessary pattern of our own perfection, we are free but not yet happy, for we are still alone. But if, while accepting the commandments, as men, because they are the pattern of perfection, we yet obey them primarily because we are living in love, then we are fully free and fully happy, we are both man and child.

Christian morality tells us what we must be. We must be whole. If we are whole, or trying to be whole, we shall act in a certain way, the way of love and worship. If we love and worship, we shall refrain from acting in ways that hurt love and destroy worship. That is the Christian order. Our Lord did not say, "I am come that you may have a code of ethics," though He told us much about the way we should act; He said, "I am come that you may have life, and have it more abundantly."

The moral way is the way of rebirth. The new life is given chiefly through the sacraments; to receive it adequately and respond to it, we must be men of prayer and virtue; the power is from God, but God waits upon our will.

We must be men of prayer. Some people think that prayer just means asking for things, and if they fail to receive exactly what they asked for, they think the whole thing a fraud. Prayer does mean asking, though it means far more than that; but it must be not the proud self but the lover who asks. The lover may ask for gifts; but he will not want to ask against the will of the other, and he will not want to ask for gifts that would hurt love; he cannot, because his deepest wants are not his own. There is nothing very mysterious, still less is there anything superstitious, about the kind of prayer that is asking, if you accept the idea that there is spiritual energy and power as well as physical, and that the first can and does influence the second. Spiritual power unaided—the power of a personality—can produce physical changes in men and cause them to act uncharacteristically in this way or in that; and similarly the power of spirit in the universe may be taken to be capable of influencing physical events. One thing is immovable, being perfect, the will of God; but we do not suppose that prayer can alter God's providence, we believe that God's providence includes the power of prayer among the many converging influences which, under His will, produce events. What is superstitious is to suppose that prayer can, in fact, compel God's will, to suppose that prayer is magic, to suppose that if I pray for a coat, a coat will infallibly appear in my wardrobe. We pray within the design of God's providence, not against it.

But even if you take the superstition out of it, you are still far from real prayer unless you pray as a lover. "Give me this gift, but only if you want to." "Let this chalice pass from me, but not my will but thine be done." Love has such power that it can extort; but to extort is the last thing it wants to do. (That is why it is so terrible when the lover sinks back into the false selfhood which grasps and utilizes; for then he extorts; and perhaps only long after realizes he has hurt or destroyed love.) To pray is to ask as lover of God; it is also to ask as lover of the world. We are a family. Not only, "Give me this gift if you think it will be good for me," but also, "Give me this gift if you think it will be good for the family." We pray not for ourselves merely but for the world; and even when we pray for ourselves, we have to remember the good of the world.

But prayer is much more than asking. If we kept it to that, we might forget the Giver in our concern for His gifts. If we follow the example of the Church in the Mass, we shall begin with confession and penitence, the prayer of the Publican; we shall go on to adoration and praise and the still, wordless prayer of wonder;[1] and only then shall we ask, when our attention is fixed on the true Centre of the self; and even so, though we pray for our own private needs and desires, we shall remember the "Collects"—the united prayers for the united needs of the world. And indeed, just as we see things at their most real when we see them and love them in God, so our prayer is most powerful and most of value when it is gathered up into the cosmic prayer of Christ and His Church. As we take the whole world to the Mass to be offered and blessed and restored, so we take our prayer to be offered and empowered. The first thing that prayer can do for us is to make us humble: to make us realize that the source of power—the power to pray, the power to live the life of virtue—is not primarily in ourselves, but in God. When prayer has thus taught us the Christian approach to morality, we shall begin to turn the whole moral life into prayer.

The Christian life, then, is always the life of the child. Yes, indeed; but it is also and equally the life of the man. There is the twofold progress: to live more and more the life and the power of God, to grow more and more in strength and maturity of mind and will and personality. The more deeply and fully you become the Other, the more deeply and fully you become yourself. And as the ultimate purpose and motive of all activity is the giving of glory to God's love, which is also and at the same time my own perfection and happiness, so the means to the end is worshipping obedience to God's power and will within me, which is also and at the same time my own labor and effort. We believe that through baptism we

---

[1] The wordless tapestry of sound woven, in the music of the Mass, on the final syllable of the word of praise Alleluia; still more, the startling stillness that descends on a church at the elevation of the Host.

are given the power to live the life of virtue; but that I should act here and now virtuously depends on my own long and laborious efforts to translate the power into practice, to acquire the habit of so acting. We have to train ourselves to freedom, to think for ourselves and judge for ourselves and act for ourselves, for only free acts can be the material out of which the good life is fashioned; and the training consists in constantly acting as we ought so as to form the habit of acting as we ought, for acts are in the realm of doing but habits are in the realm of being, and it is only when we *are* good that we have the good life. So we become good in so far as we become free *men*; but the freedom we acquire is the freedom to obey love, the freedom to live the life of the *child*.

We believe that the moral life is the search for wholeness. Some have taught that the end in view is to become the perfectly rational man, and that the way is to suppress the passions and emotions lest they sweep like a gale through the trim temple of reason and disturb the worshippers. It is Talleyrand's *surtout point de zèle*; and the correctness of eighteenth-century religion and the eighteenth-century God. We have seen already what happens when you repress half the personality. But what a religion! You would be saying to God, "Oh yes, I worship You; but only with that portion of your handiwork which I find it possible to consider respectable." You might attempt to praise God thus: but you would stifle yourself with the starchy formalities of your illuminated address. You could praise Him with logic and science, never with timbrel and harp, never with poetry and ecstasy and ardor, never with love. Christian morality is worship: not the worship of the divine Mind by the human reason, but the worship by the whole man of the whole God. You worship with the whole man in so far as instincts, passions, emotions, mind, will are integrated and fulfilled in the unity of the personality by being "harnessed to the service of the Light." And again, how is this process brought about? By childlike obedience to the power and sharing in the life of God; by laboriously acquiring the maturity and mastery of manhood.

Virtue is defined as the enduring possession of the power to act with facility and readiness in a certain way. You can speak instead, if you will, of a "good habit"; but it is not a question of a mechanical habit in the sense of a mannerism which is often unconscious and unconsciously acquired. The musician acquires by long hard practice the enduring ability to play well; if you have acquired the habit of temperateness or generosity you will normally and spontaneously be gentle and generous. But it is more than a technique. The musician must have the technical skill; but technical skill alone does not make the musician. To bring the technique to life, you must have music in the soul. Vision without skill is dumb; but skill without vision is dead. So with the moral virtues: there is the acquired skill, but underneath the skill, the vision. You must know the presence of God in the soul.

First, then, maturity of mind, mastery, autonomy: not the proud, assumed autonomy of the false self which tries to master God, but the real autonomy of the man who has learnt to master himself. You must acquire knowledge, you must be critical and learn to judge, you must be able to make up your own mind, you must try to be wise: because the judgment, "This is the right action and not that," must rest, in the last resort, with that power in the mind to make practical moral decisions which we call conscience. Then you find the four great modes of right action—prudence, justice, fortitude, temperateness—as elements in every virtuous action; but these things are the possession of the mature personality;

they mean the exercise of reason, courage and control. And each particular virtue in its turn means a similar mastery of the particular material involved. The man of virtue is master and maker; for he has mastered the material of life and acquired the art of living.

But behind the skill, the vision. The temperate man is usually absolved from the labor of reasoning out how to act temperately here and now; he knows by a kind of instinct; and he knows because he not only has tenderness and the humility of the flesh, but is humble and tender. So you find in him a childlike freshness and spontaneity that are denied to the purely rational man.

Then again, all virtue is grounded in humility and is a mode of worship; and again you have the dependence and smallness of the child.

There is a third thing. The moral life as a whole is rooted in the life shared directly with God, the life of faith, hope and love. And by faith we are led, not against reason but beyond reason, to the knowledge of God in Himself and therefore of ourselves. By hope we are kept young of heart; for it teaches us to trust in God, to work with all our energy but to leave the future to Him: it gives us poverty of spirit and so saves us from solicitude. And by love we are not told about God, we are brought to Him; we are brought down into the depths of the soul to become one with Him there, to learn through sorrow and repentance to be reborn and say, "It is Thyself"; and then it drives us out again to rediscover the world and to make all men and things our brothers, to show us the unity of the family of creation: and so we have still more emphatically the affirmation that God is the centre and that, if we live, we live in Him.

And then, finally, there is the direct influence and impulsion of the Spirit upon the soul; for though the power of God that is given us is expressed through the virtues, the vitality of the virtues themselves is limited by the fact that they are the possession of finite human mind and will. We try to hold the infinite in human hands. We see as in a glass, darkly; however fervent the faithful Christian, there is an imperfection in faith itself because in itself it is obscure; there is an imperfection in the moral life because the apprehension of the good is limited in itself by the narrow compass of the human mind. But as the wind that bloweth where it listeth, so is everyone that is born of the Spirit: it is the breath of the Spirit that gives us the freedom of the sons of God because it raises human action above the confines of the purely human. All the powers of the personality will be given this enlightening and energizing impulse if we can learn to accept and respond to it: the mind's darkness illumined by a direct experience of God, an intuitive perception of divine truth, a sense of the Christian life both in theory and in action; the moral life deepened and strengthened by an immediately God-given sense of worship and reverence, and by a child-like confidence that is proof against all dangers, together with an "insatiable desire" to overcome them all in His service.

Here, when this direct loving obedience to the Spirit is perfect (for here, too, God waits upon our will), we have the fullness of the moral life, the immensity of power and personality of the Christian saint. Think for a moment of a type of man with whom we are too familiar. At his most characteristic he is somewhat stout and red of face from heavy food; he is capable in office or shop or factory; when he leaves it he likes a good meal, though he is hardly discriminating; he reads the paper or glances at a magazine or two; he likes a tot of whisky, though he is inclined to bolt it a little thought-lessly; he may while away the time uncritically at a cinema; if he talks about anything at all outside his own immediate work or pleasures, he will probably repeat in slightly garbled form the political views of his morning paper; he calls his friends "old boy" and his wife "old girl," and if he is what is known as a clean-living man he will probably develop an irritability or some other mild form of mental or physical disorder which he will ascribe to business anxieties; he will never get to know his son and daughter and would find it impossible if he tried, and when he is dying he will possibly shed a secret tear or two over his dog, whom he has never understood either. Could we say that this was a moral life? We could not, for the simple reason that it was not a life at all. Morality is a sort of life, not a sort of death.

If ever we feel forced to conclude that the great majority of a nation is like this, we shall have to conclude also that the nation is doomed. It is possible to be dead in every sense that matters and still go on catching the train to the office in the morning. When a whole nation does that, it is better perhaps that it should do the thing thoroughly. Thank God, there are still an enormous number who have not had life and wisdom smothered and killed by what is called education. The other day in a village inn an old man spoke to me of the farmlands in the village and the quality of the soil and the way the fields were being ruthlessly torn and plundered and left in ruin by the men who wanted the iron ore and had no concern for the land; he spoke with knowledge and sense and wisdom; he did not know about the land merely, he knew the land, he had the feel of the land in his soul, he was alive. Thank God, there are still many like him. But he was old.

"I have said, Ye are gods." And yet we have known men

who were dead though the fact had not occurred to them; and we have seen squalor and stupidity and the pettiness that poisons and kills. Where are these gods? Look at the saints. We think of gods as having a greater intensity of life, a greater power and a greater freedom than we. And here in the saints we have the "insatiable desire" for meeting difficulties and braving angers; we have the "hunger and thirst after justice"; we have the charity that reaches to the ends of the world; we have the fullest possible intensity of life because we have the infinity of the life and power of God. The man who is dead in spirit was once alive when he was a child and was one with the universe; and here we have the complete obedience to the Spirit, the power to see with the eyes of God and judge with the mind of God and desire with the will of God which mean that the life of the child is preserved and fulfilled in the heart of the saint. We think of the gods as having a greater intensity of life than we. And here we have the fullness of a life that is whole; a life in which instincts and emotions and desires and thought and will are all gathered up and given a more than human vitality by being made to share in the life and express and fulfil the purposes of the Infinite. We think of the gods as having a greater power than we; and here we have the faith that moves mountains, the strength that laughs at perils, the love that sweeps like a gale wind through the world because it is one with the Love that is a burning and a consuming fire. We think of the gods as having a greater freedom than we. And here we have the freedom that always does what it wants; the freedom that has gone beyond the freedom from the slavery of sin and the pseudo-self, beyond the bondage of the law which seems like an external restraint because it is obeyed only from fear, beyond the clash of finite with infinite will, because we have here the man who has found that the heart is only fully free when it is living in love, and that then it is free because there are no longer two wills but only one. "I am come that you may have *life*, and have it more abundantly."

At the summit of the moral life you come to the point where lover and master, child and man, the man of vision and the man of power, meet and are one. And in so doing, you come also to the answer of the greatest paradox that confronts the moralist. "If I seek for virtue I seek for my own perfection; but if I seek for my own perfection I am selfish, and selfishness is the essence of vice." It is an argument that seems to hold against the ethic of Aristotle; it will not hold against the morality that is worship. When you speak of love, you cannot really distinguish giving from getting, for each is indistinguishably both. You cannot take the desire for joy out of love without destroying it; but the desire for joy is itself a desire to give, and the joy is desired only provided that it is a gift. *Nihil unquam in te nisi te exquisivi*; when you seek virtue you desire God, who is your joy; but the more deeply you are living in love, the more fully you will live in Him, and therefore, even though you more and more desire your own happiness with Him, you will more and more think of your happiness in terms of serving Him.

The end of the moral life is wholeness. But it is wholeness of life; and life is creative energy. All living is seeing and loving; but all living is also making. The vision of the artist impels him to express what he has seen; the love of the lover impels him to give. The man who is dead in spirit is not dead merely because only a minute fragment of his personality exists; he is dead because he leaves the world unenlarged. The morality which is worship is both vision and love; and you cannot see it fully unless you see it as it affects the world. The whole human being is more than an individual body-spirit, a closed system: he is an individual in an environment, and on every level he is related by a thousand bonds to that environment, which he must affect for good or for ill. To be just or temperate is to deal justly or temperately with persons and things. If you are unjust and cruel, you may ruin another human life; if you are gentle and generous, you may make it enduringly happy. We are individuals in an environment; we are individuals in an environment which is largely in the power of evil, and for which we are largely responsible. Morality, then, is worship; but that sort of worship which fulfils in the world the purposes of God. This is the insatiable desire of the saints: to help to restore the world to God. It is not enough to be all things; we have to help and to restore all things. It is not enough to "realize the idea of the Good" in our own lives: we have to realize the idea of the good in our environment. For indeed, the Good we have to express in our lives is God; and God is self-diffusive Love.

The morality which is ultimately self-centered is of necessity individualist also—even the service of others can be a form of selfishness; but the morality which is God-centered, though it necessarily involves the perfection of the self, looks directly to the purposes of God. So when we think of the moral life from God's side, in terms of the giving of His power and life through the sacramental system, we cannot forget that this power is given not for ourselves alone. The Church's office is to bring the truth and the life of God to the world, to restore it; sometimes this power is given to individuals entirely for the sake of others; you read in the New Testament of the gifts of "tongues" and prophecy and the

86

rest, which served and empowered the Church as a whole; you read especially of the gift of healing, the healing of body and soul alike, by prayer and the laying on of hands; and still to-day the Church's office and privilege is to bless and to heal—to bless the earth and the fruits of the earth, to bless the animals, to bless mankind, and to heal the sick in body and mind, to heal by prayer and blessing, to heal through the liturgy which has such power to restore and integrate the unconscious, to heal through the touch of the waters at Lourdes where faith makes whole. But that is not all. The life and power that are given to the individual for the individual are given to the man in his environment, are given to the man as taking part in the cosmic struggle, and so are given in their turn for the blessing and healing of all things.

Think first of baptism. It gives us the new life, which to say precisely that it frees us from the bondage of the spirit of evil and makes it possible for us to live and work for the purposes of God. Its first concern is with the individual personality; but we necessarily affect our environment not only by what we do but by what we are; and as baptism creates in us the responsibility of being members of the Church, the responsibility of being lovers of one another, so it gives us the power to fulfil our responsibilities.

Faith is life, for it means living in God; but the life of God is something that has to be slowly and painfully realized in us—we have to do and experience in our own way what Christ did and experienced for us; and this personal progress is part of a much vaster cosmic process, the long travail whereby the world as a whole must learn eventually to "put on Christ" and to be made whole. As we are dependent on and determined by the past, so we, in our own lives, fashion the future. Just as we ourselves in the present are weakened (because the Church is weakened) by every individual betrayal and strengthened (because the Church is strengthened) by every individual fidelity, so if we succeed in realizing the life of God within us we build up the future, if we fail we destroy.

What Christ did for us, we in our own way must do. If you are a Christian, you must be a mediator. Living in union with Christ, you must labor to bring the life and power of Christ into the world to which you are bound by the solidarity of sin; the Church, like the individual, is not a closed system, but a power and an energy that come from God and go out to the world in order to bring the two together; by baptism you are made a sharer in the power and the energy, and, therefore, in the work that has to be done.

The sacraments correspond to the deep enduring needs and also to the great landmarks of human life. Baptism is the sacrament of rebirth, the sacrament of the child. Confirmation is the sacrament of the youth approaching manhood, about to face the world as an independent person. He will have to face a world that is largely hostile to his true self; he may have to face an environment that will oppose all his deepest desires and dreams; and he will have to be strong if he is to resist submersion and retain his independence. This sacrament of strengthening is given us to bring about the victory of independence; it is given us to make us spiritually adult also. Catholics speak of the Church as a mother: her motherhood is the correlative of the humility of the child; but just as the growth of human life implies a growth of independence, of the power to make one's own life, so too we become spiritually adult in so far as we arrive at maturity of judgment and conscience and the ability to play our own part in the cosmic struggle on the side of the good—serving the Church and not merely relying on her.[2] Hence the symbolism of this sacrament: oil denoting strength and the warrior spirit, the anointing on the forehead for courage, the tap on the cheek for endurance of hardship and suffering, the pentecostal fire which symbolizes growth as the water of baptism symbolizes birth. We are come to the fullness of social responsibility; we are to be masters and makers and not merely children; we are to bring holiness to others by being holy ourselves, to set others on fire by contact with the fire within us.

So the sacrament of confirmation is associated with the old traditional idea of the common priesthood of the laity: the official sharing in the priestly power and office of Christ. If you are looking for the essential meaning of the Church, do not stop short at the organization, the legal and juridical aspects, do not isolate the teaching authority, for this, too, is only a part: you will find the essential meaning of the Church and its claims when you see it as a torrent of life and power—the life and power that teach and sanctify and rule—descending from God to man.

The Church is essentially Christ living and acting in the world. But we must think of Christ as the "total Christ": Christ acting in and through the authority and power of the Church, and thence in and through the whole family of Christians. So that if His power is not opposed but on the contrary more and more fully recognized and received by the Christian—received precisely through loving obedience to the Church—then the Christian is fully a Christian at last because at last he is bearing the Christ within him out into the world which as yet knows not Christ; he is living the Christian life in something of its fullness because he is receiv-

[2] Cf. Chapter VIII.

ing from Christ in the Church the life and power that can restore the world, and turning with love to the task of restoring it. Notice how at the first Pentecost it is not to individuals merely but to the Christian family that the Spirit comes, and comes as fire: it is the bringing of a common power for this common task—the task of restoring all things in Christ.

But unhappily, we can never think of the cosmic struggle as though it were a clearly defined battle between the forces of good and the forces of evil. It is waged by the Church; but it is waged also within the Church. We betray what we love. We try to fight for the restoration of the world, for the coming of the kingdom; but the coming is postponed, and the power of the Church to heal and make holy is curtailed, by the persisting presence and power of evil within us. My personal sins reinforce the power of evil; but I am responsible for more than this. We are one in the love and life of God, but we are one also in the solidarity of sin. Whenever I sin I first of all weaken the Church; and through that weakening there are other sins, and I am in part responsible for them. But the mercy of God will repair this damage too. We see the sacrament of penance in its fullness and greatness if we see it thus against the background of the total struggle. It has as its first purpose to restore the individual to life in God; but it is medicinal also to the life of the Church as a whole. We retard the Church's work by our sins; we help it on by our use of this sacrament—building up our own health and power we help to build up the corporate health and power of the community of Christians also.

Penance is the sacrament of healing, the healing of the individual for the strengthening of the Church. It is not a negative thing—the wiping out of something that is past; the past is never abolished. Its whole purpose is positive and creative. Just as personal sin repeats over again the primal sin, so penance repeats the work of baptism: freeing us from the power of evil, restoring us to the Church, strengthening us to overcome the weakness that sin leaves in us, so that we may work again in the Church for the victory of the Good. But the cross must precede the resurrection. Penance is given us not to lull us into a feeling that all is well, but to shake us from complacency into self-knowledge, into a realization of our responsibility for the continuing power of evil in the world, into a deeper realization of God's love for humanity and the shallowness and unreality of our love for Him. We can fight for the world only when the sense of sin has turned our half-hearted repentance into the sorrow of love, shown us to what extent we are traitors to God's purposes, and so caused us to begin with humility to put our trust not in ourselves but in Him. Unless the grain of wheat die, itself remaineth alone.

But after the death, the resurrection; after sorrow and repentance, the life and power of the living Bread. There follows the greatest of all the sacraments, which brings us not divine power merely, but the Source of divine power. It is the Eucharist above all which empowers us to fight for the Good, and to fight as a family. There are the two dangers: of independence in isolation, the man without the child; and of uniformity without maturity, the child without the man. The Eucharist is the supreme way to wholeness. The Mass is first of all a sacrifice, an affirmation that God and not the false self is the centre; it is the sacrifice of the whole man gathered up into the sacrifice of the whole Church, which itself is gathered up into the sacrifice of Christ; and then again it is the sacrament which effects the oneness first of all of the individual with Christ and then of the family of Christians with one another—the Communion is preceded by the kiss of peace, as it was preceded in the primitive Church by the *agape*, the love-feast. When the Mass is over and the *Ite missa est* is said, it is not simply a number of individuals who are sent out to serve and restore the world: it is a family.

True, a family is a unity, not a uniformity: there is diversity of gifts, even though the same Spirit; the first thing the Eucharist effects is the wholeness of the individual Christian. But it is the sacrificed Christ who is received; and it is part of the purpose of the receiving that through it the Body of Christ should be built up in love and unity, and that, through the unity of the Body, the restoring power of Christ should be made visible and active in the world.

What a tragedy when the immensity of this coming of the Infinite into the soul is made a purely individual thing and we forget the family! How can we fail to note the insistence of the liturgy or the fact that it is our *common* sacrifice that we are offering, and the *common* sacrament that we are receiving, a sacrament of unity symbolized in the kiss of peace; and how can we fail to realize that, when we come down from the altar after the Communion, it is in a wholly new and richer sense that we are "all one in that One!" But what a tragedy also if we forget the larger family of creation!

When a Christian is sick and bed-ridden it is the office of the priest to bring the sacramental Christ to the house; and the preparations that are made, the solemnity of the reception of the priest who bears the Host, enact once again the humility and wonder of the Centurion, "Lord, I am not worthy that Thou shouldst enter under my roof." But we do not always notice that, when we come down from the altar and return into our houses, the same thing is done; we in our turn are God-bearers; and if it must be with a new sense of reverence and a new sense of oneness that we salute one another, we cannot but remember also the thing that is done in and to the world. How terrible if we allow ourselves to sink back into the pettinesses that kill love and oneness, how terrible if we fail to find courage to meet and conquer the spirit of hatred and evil, since we bear within us the power of the presence of the Good Himself! How terrible if we are content to leave mankind in its loneliness, when we bear within us Him who came to take away the sin and, therefore, the loneliness of the world!

We are all meant to be mediators. But we need not think it necessarily our duty to be forever attempting to argue these things; we need never think it our duty to preach at others; nothing is more depressing and more illogical than aggressive Christianity; we preach as we ought if we are what we ought to be, and we preach best if we are what we most ought to be, a family living in love and in God. To the sacrament of marriage, with all that it has to tell us of the duties and power of love in the world, we turn later; but the root of the matter is already here. "See how these Christians love one another." If we who are Christians could make the world say the words again as it said them first, with awe and wonder, we should have fulfilled the first part of our work as Christians; and the second would follow automatically, for we could not to that extent love one another without loving the world.

But we shall not so love one another if, in fact, we adopt a selfish sectarian attitude to the world. When men see that the building of the Church is a labor of love, the labor of a family, and that it is the building not of a fortress but of a home whose doors are always open, an invitation to enjoy the light and warmth within; when they see that we are ready to live and die for one another because we know that our duty together as family is to live and die for the world Christ came to restore, then they will begin to say seriously that Christianity is love in practice as well as in theory, and if they look for Christ they will not dismiss the possibility of finding Him, despite our sinfulness, in our midst.

The way back to God is the way of worship, the worship given by the whole human being, man and child, to God. But the whole human being precisely as such does not worship alone. When you are living in love you cannot live alone, you cannot think or will or act alone; when you live in Christ you think and will and act in Christ, and it is the "total Christ," it is Christ as gathering to Himself the totality of created things. In the prayers of thanksgiving after Mass is included the canticle, "Bless the Lord, *all* ye works of the Lord." We go back to God in company with those we love, helped and helping. To help all created things, that is the measure of our responsibility; to be helped by all, that is the measure of our hope. Do you think it childish and superstitious to look for help to the saints or the angels? We look to our friends for help; what is childish is to suppose that we cannot be helped except by things or persons we can see or touch. We live in the world of space and time, but we live in eternity too, in the eternal present; the world is a haunted house, but not all the spirits that inhabit it are mournful ghosts or spirits of evil; the mystery of iniquity is offset by the glory of the communion of saints. Do you think that the mother who dies is no longer in contact with her children, that lover is hopelessly separated from lover? And these great ones of God set no limit to their love of those who at any moment of our time-world are trying to play their part in the cosmic struggle. The modern West has reached a chilly cerebral stage in its evolution; think how it might be helped and perhaps saved from complete desiccation by the might of the seraphs, those spirits whom Christian tradition associates especially with fire, with the burning love which is the prayer of wonder.

We begin to live the moral life in the Christian sense when we begin to turn all that we do and are into worship; and if we do that, the false self will die within us, and we shall begin to be made whole; and we shall forget to be grasping, even about the things of the spirit, because we shall want to serve the world. But in fact we shall walk in all the power of God and His saints and angels, we shall walk in the company of all who love Him and of all the things He loves, and so we shall reach the breadth and height and depth of the infinite skies, and lose our fear of what can hurt us and our fear of what we can lose, and beneath all the pain of the world that is in us—for nothing now will suffer without our suffering too—there will be the unquenchable joy of the saints.

Then there will be only the final consummation to wait for, when, in the company of those who have loved and helped us and those we have loved and served, we shall enter into the ultimate fullness of integrity, we shall see Him as He is and all things in Him in their glory, and so we shall know at last the complete oneness for which we have been so long unsuccessfully striving because in the fullness of the vision of the Godhead we shall find at last that there is nothing that we cannot love.

PART II
MAN THE MAKER

V

The Making of Art

In the beginning, God planted a garden. He is Lover and Creator; and He made man in His own image, to be lover and maker in his turn. There is evil in the world and so the garden is no longer given; we have to conquer thorns and thistles and make the garden before we can begin to dress it and keep it; but it is still our destiny to be gardeners, and to be gardeners for God.

We want to be lovers, we want to be makers. The two things are dependent on one another. If we are living in love with the world, we shall have joy in the beauty of the world; if we are living in love with the world, we shall also want to make beauty in and for the world. If we are living in love with God, we shall rejoice; but we shall also want to be makers for His glory. Love is more than a state of being: it is an impulsion to act and to make. Of necessity the lover brings gifts; the lover traditionally sings. It is part of the process whereby we become whole. We find the true self by becoming what lies about us and beyond us; but we find the true self in its fullness when our love for what lies about and beyond us impels us to create. You have seen or known the desire of lovers to imitate God and make another being in their own image and likeness; you have seen or known how the artist is forced to express what he sees and loves. But we are all meant in one way or another to be lovers and artists: if we were not, we should cease to exist in God's image and

99

likeness, we should be dead. If we are to be made whole, we must learn to be makers; but to learn to be makers we must learn to love. There is no true art without reverence; every song worth singing is in some sense a love-song.

We live in a world which has lost art and beauty in its daily life because it has forgotten how to love and worship. We live in a world which smashes and grabs; and you see its symbol in those magazine covers which are the direct denial of art as well as of prudence because they come not from the vision and love of beauty but from a cold commercial calculation of the sales value of an appeal to sentiment or sensuality. We live in a world which values things for their utility and primarily for their commercial utility; and you see its symbol in the fact that the national feasts have been degraded into things called bank holidays. What could be more sub-human than a society in which a few produce an art which is intelligible only to a few, and the vast majority are condemned to a life of drudgery punctuated by the negative respite of a bank holiday?

If you are not making, you cannot possibly be happy, because it is the destiny of every man to be a maker. Do not think of art in terms of painting, sculpture, poems, music and no more: art is simply the skill and vision to make lovely things, and is there anything in the world of man that could not and ought not to be lovely? From cooking and sewing to statecraft, from ploughing or town-planning to music and song, all the ways of making are modes of art, and are meant to rejoice the hearts of men. In the beginning, God planted a garden; it was left to commercial enterprise to plant a slum.

We are all meant to be makers; and the instinct to make lies deep in us. See what happens when the instinct is thwarted and the personality robbed of its wholeness. You cannot kill an

100

instinct; you can only repress it for a time; and if you rob it of
fulfilment it will have its revenge. It is man's destiny first to
love and then by love to master and mould his environment;
and if you prevent him, if you take his art from him, you will
eventually take his love away also, and he will forget how to
see; but you will not kill the original instinct, and it will find
another outlet, and all the energy and skill that should have
been used in molding material things into loveliness in the
service of love will be used sooner or later in destruction in
the service of hate.

The real artist is concerned about money, yes; he is concerned about his daily bread. But he is even more concerned
about the work in itself and the beauty of it and its rightness
for the human environment for which it is destined. And so
we find that penury and hunger will not turn him aside from
his chosen work; we find that his work makes him happy
because it is enlarging him and making him whole. But if we
take men's birthright from them and make them forget it, and
force them to give their lives to what is not a form of making
but a form of dull half-human doing, then they will be
unhappy, and sooner or later there will be an explosion: they
will enlarge themselves by force and in hatred and blindly, not
knowing what they want, and so we shall have crimes of cruelty and violence, we shall have economic unrest and piracy
and competition, we shall have the political horrors of nationalism, hatred and war.

Thank God, the world can never kill our creativeness
entirely; there are forms of making it cannot touch; which
explains the greatness of the ordinary men and women
against whom the modern world of the West has sinned so
terribly. We may be robbed of our right to make beauty in
our daily work; there remains the making of beauty in our

daily life. There remains the making of love and friendship and good fellowship; and even if that is taken from us, there remains the inner making of the soul.

We live in a world which is ugly because it is built and controlled so largely by the men of power. There is no art without reverence. But where you have reverence—the reverence of the man of vision for things and persons alike—then you will have more than just art and beauty: you will have an art that is socially responsible and that plays its part in the cosmic struggle.

You will have art; because to make lovely things is the right of every human being, and where you have a society built on reverence for the human being, you will have that right respected. Every man is meant to be a maker; but every man is a unique personality, and has his own particular type and way of making; and if you dragoon men and treat them as units, whether in political life or in industry, you are to that extent killing them, and ultimately killing the society in which they live. The garden is no longer given; there is drudgery. The men of power are unmoved by the drudgery of millions, and the machines which could have reduced it have, in fact, reduced it for the fortunate few only by multiplying it for the many; for the many are made the unwilling servants of power and profit.

But a world built on reverence would have gone to work very differently. There would be drudgery, but the inventive genius of man would have reduced it; there would still be drudgery, but it would be equally shared; it would be equally shared, not in order that there might be endless leisure in which to do nothing, but in order that every man might have time and opportunity to devote his life to a form of making.

Mistrust those who talk of drudgery as something God-given which we should not seek to escape: it is part of the wages of sin, but we are here not to accept sin but to overcome it, to restore the garden by the sweat of our brow. Drudgery is soul-destroying because it is uncreative; we are here to restore the world, and one of the ways of restoring the world is to restore the creativeness of work. But mistrust those also who talk of the leisure state, the elimination of hard work, as the goal at which we should aim: they are preaching a doctrine of death. Leisure is of its essence a secondary thing; it exists only to offset our main creative work, to renew and refresh us for it—and even so, there is something very wrong about a world which spends its leisure exclusively in passive amusement. We are fully men only if our life as a whole is a form of making, not just a number of little hobbies: we need something big enough to occupy our energies for a lifetime. Mistrust them when they talk about abolishing hard work; if you abolish hard work, you abolish making, and then you will be miserable. Drudgery is not an evil because it is hard but because it is uncreative; and making which is not hard is likely to be of little value, because it is hard to find the vision and acquire the skill, and it is endlessly hard to express the vision when you have found it.

But there is one thing that can redeem even drudgery and make it creative: to do it for love. It will become itself a form of making, because it is precisely a making of love. And when the work is already art you thus become doubly a maker: for in the same act you are making beauty and making love. So it is that art can help in the restoring of the world. If you work not only because you love the thing you are making but also because you love the world for which you are making it, you will be helping it by restoring its vision, but you will be doing more than that. Art is an extension of the personality;

and as a personality can influence others by being even more than by saying or doing, so the work done carries within itself something of the being and the influence of the maker. If you love men, your work will lead all but the willfully blind to love men in their turn; if you love justice, tenderness, courage, your work will speak of these things. And again, there is more than that. Art is the making of beauty and the serving of humanity; it is also the worship of God. People sometimes think it foolish to reverence the relics of the saints; yet it is only an extension of the deep instinct that is in us to keep and cherish the things that belonged to those we love. But it is something more. "And Jesus said: Somebody hath touched me; for I know that virtue is gone out from me." But it was the hem of His garment that she had touched. There is a holiness and a power in the things that belong to holy people. If your making is worship, if you make because you love what you set out to make and because you love men, but most of all because you love God, then you will be trebly a maker, and your work will serve humanity because it will help to lead humanity back to God.

Think of some very humble and ordinary form of making, like the sewing of a patch on a coat. You can regard it as drudgery, and do it with careless or perhaps with savage impatience; and then you turn it into a job. (And when you find a society like our own, where the young are forced to look for a job so as to have enough money to live on, then you can know that there is rottenness deep down in it. We should not have to make money an end and drudgery the means to it; we should be able to make art the end and money, as a matter of course, its by-product. We should not have to work in order to live; we should be able to live in order to make.)

You can regard the patch very differently. You can do it with pride in your workmanship, so that it becomes a thing of beauty; then you are already an artist. You can do it with love, and so turn it into love-making; and then you are twice an artist. You can do it as an act of worship of God—"I patch this coat for this poor child for whom I am forever responsible, as a part of our life together that You have given us and that we turn into worship of You"—and then you are three times an artist; you are completely alive. And why should not every action that you do be like this? But we are enslaved by a system that despises art and has no room for love and reverence; and so we can be excused if we think sometimes that

the end draws near; the soil is stale.

Unless there can be a rebirth our world is doomed; and it must be a rebirth of reverence.

Reverence produces art; but art, in its turn, produces reverence: reverence for the world, for men, for God. It can lead us to the steps of the temple. So it is that poetry was defined as that which does not save the soul, indeed, but makes the soul worth saving. The perfect work is worship, an expression of the sense of the holy; and can lead the beholder to worship in his turn. In itself art is autonomous; it can accept no laws but the laws of art itself, the needs of the work; and beauty can serve and help humanity, though it may well be dangerous, no matter what the moral theory or judgment, the motive or intention, that lie behind it. But it is not art that makes things for us, it is the artist; and the artist is not autonomous. He will serve humanity best if he accepts the subordination not of art in itself but of human art to worship and holiness: he will serve humanity best if what he makes is holy.

105

What is a holy picture? Some people would say it is a picture which represents Christ or the saints. But there are representations of Christ and the saints which are far from holy; and there are pictures which have in them a sense of the holy but represent quite other things. You can use a holy theme as your subject but glorify only what is in the Gospel sense worldly: you can glorify all that the men of power stand for; you can glorify yourself. There are plenty of examples of these pictures which represent the holy but glorify humanity apart from God; there are plenty of buildings and sculptures and books. They are filled not with the sense of worship but with the sense of power; and it explains the strident vulgarity of their grandiosities. They lack humor because by definition they lack humility. You may begin with the Mona Lisa; you will end with the Mayor of Puddlecombe. But if you reverence men because you live with them in God and know the presence of God within them, the sense of holiness will be in your vision, and your work will be worship, and whatever you paint, you will paint a holy picture. Then you will be helping to restore the world because you will be helping to restore its beauty; you will be helping to restore man's dominion over matter—his true dominion, the dominion of love; you will be helping to restore his sense of worship; you will be helping to restore his wholeness, because you will be helping to restore him to God.

Art speaks to us in symbol. In so far as a world without art is a world without symbol it will drive us mad, as so many are being driven mad in the world of today. For the part of the personality that lives in the realm of symbol is staved and suppressed and finally driven to live a life of its own, unrelated to the life of every day and in defiance of it; and that way madness lies. If you worship God as a maker, you worship in

106

wholeness; for art calls forth the whole personality, reason, intuition, senses, feeling, whether you think of the one who makes or of the one who enjoys. In the work of art there is order, clarity, proportion, things which appeal to the reason; there is the surface rational meaning, though it is secondary to the work as art. There is appeal to feeling also; for beauty involves not a cold, objective judgment of truth or falsehood but a judgment of value, the correlative of desire or love. There is appeal to senses and intuition, and it is the essence of the beautiful; for the thing is seen and becomes one with the beholder by an intuitive awareness which is experienced precisely in and through the senses. It is not simply the mind that experiences and lives; it is the whole "I."

There is more than that. Art speaks to us in symbol; it is not a statement of fact (except in a secondary way), but an evocation of a deep awareness and a deep-rooted dream. Every song is ultimately a love-song; and love is both knowledge and desire. When you come to the greatest art, you are in touch with more than an individual, you are in the realm of the universal; for the artist speaks for more than himself, he is beyond the particularities of style and race and period, he expresses not only his own desires and vision but humanity's secular dreams.

That is why the archetype of all art is the Church's liturgy. When you have a people living in the symbolism and responding to the rhythm of the Church's liturgy, you have a people living and worshipping in wholeness, because at every level they are healthily alive. They may be poor and downtrodden and deprived of many of their rights as men; they may be ignorant and uncivilized, and the things they make may be crude. But underneath all that there is a health and a sanity which are denied to a commercialized and, therefore, warped civilization; there is a wholeness which is denied to the individualist, however cultured; there is a deep and perhaps unconscious creativeness which is denied to the most finished craftsman who works only at the surface level of his mind. The liturgy fulfils the reason, for it is doctrine that it expresses; it speaks in symbol, and evokes an intuitive response; it is addressed to the senses, for its materials are color, gesture, perfume, sound; and it tells of the Truth, but of the Truth who is also the Good and the Beautiful. If you are living within it, you are brought constantly to the Eternal; but you are in touch, too, with the rhythm of earth and sun and stars, the endless cycle of death and renewal. You cannot remain enclosed in your narrow selfhood, for you are living a corporate act which itself expresses a greater community since it expresses the dreams of humanity, the desire of the universe; you will never be uncreative, for you are caught up in and molded by this endless process of the making of the wholeness of man. Every time you bow or raise the hand or move in harmony with the ritual pattern, every time you sing to God or respond to the voice of the priest, every time your eye follows the flame of the candle or the wreathing of smoke from the thurible, you are not merely doing something but becoming something: you are entering into the life of God and of His whole creation, you are also learning, deep in your soul, to make.

Compare what happens when the liturgy is destroyed or forgotten. It will disintegrate, like love, into its two components; and when they are isolated from one another they become destructive, they diminish instead of enlarging the soul. Instead of a creative act of worship, you will have sentiment and sensuality. And notice that these things are in their essence the opposite of worship, because in their essence they are simply the indulgence of the false self. Instead of the great universal symbols for the deepest desires and realities, you will find pettiness, a shallow escape. You will find music that begins by exalting humanity and ends by defiling it, because it has forgotten that its office here is only to be a symbol of the Inexpressible. You will find the eye and ear involved not in the virile grandeur and glory of an epiphany but in a sensual indulgence which ignores the spirit, because there is nothing behind these sights and sounds which could speak to the spirit. You will find the immensities of religion, of humanity's needs and humanity's destiny, set aside; and in their place there will be only the thoughts that soothe and lull the individual—a lace-edged, flower-strewn covering over the mouth of hell. And finally you will find the idea of making discarded altogether, and replaced by a purely passive self-indulgent receptivity: and discarded because radically the idea of worship itself is discarded, the Mass no longer a cosmic corporate act but a sort of spectacle for which one can take seats as for a show. And then people think that the effort to restore the liturgy is an aesthetic preoccupation of purists—when it is a fight to bring back the stuff of life.

Art speaks to us in symbol. Some people think that if it is to be morally justifiable, it must preach some explicit message: a book must have an edifying theme, a picture must convey a pious sentiment, presumably a table or a chair must somehow embody a moral text. All preaching ought to be art (which is not the same as saying that it ought to be oratory); but that does not mean that all art ought to be preaching. If you set out to preach in your paint or stone or music, you will destroy your work. Art uses symbol to bring us awareness of reality; it teaches, but not by argument, not by trying to compel the reason; it can draw aside a veil, but if we are willfully blind it can do nothing for us. If we have eyes to see, it can teach us a little how to live, not by telling us, but by showing us something of what life can be and ought to be.

In that way it can teach us to love and worship; and the greatest art, and above all the liturgy, can teach us to love and worship as a family. In the Middle Ages men were cultural communists; what mattered to them was not who had written the book or painted the picture, still less the problem of copyright, but the fact that the world had been enriched, the human family had been helped a little further to the recovery of its vision. In itself the later evolution of interest in the artist as a personality is good; but the world of the men of power has left its mark here also. If you think of art as the prerogative of a few, it is natural to think of it as a purely personal affair of the artist's, to transfer the autonomy of art in itself to the artist, and to absolve him from social responsibility. But it cannot be done. You cannot make as a man unless you make, at least indirectly, for humanity. You may make for yourself, you may make for a particular person; but what you make and the mode of your making must ultimately affect the struggle of good and evil because they must be ultimately the worship either of the false self or of God. In what we make just as much as in what we do, we are each responsible for all.

A terrible responsibility rests upon the artists in the narrower sense, the painters and poets and makers of music, in a world like our own which has so largely forgotten art in its daily life. If they deliberately turn their treasure into a toy, if they deliberately address themselves to a cultured clique and ignore and despise the masses as past redemption, they are fighting on the side of evil because they are refusing their responsibility to the world. If they use their power to deify humanity or to deify themselves, they are fighting on the side of evil because they are leading men to idolatry instead of to wholeness, they are reinforcing instead of fighting the original sin.

But this is not a responsibility that we can limit to the fine arts; we are all meant to be makers, and it rests upon us all. We can accept the idea of passive amusement and the leisure state and pretend that making does not matter; or we can pretend that making is not dependent on vision and love; in either case we oppose and hinder the restoring of humanity. Not by what we say but by what we are do we acquiesce in an art-less world; and if we do, we betray humanity. We can acquiesce in a world without worship; and again we betray humanity. There are some indeed, who deliberately relinquish their birthright in order to serve humanity more fully; who take on themselves the cross of an inhuman industrialism in order to redeem industrialism, to restore it from within. They are turning drudgery into creation on a higher plane. They are fighting for art and for life in the camp of the enemy. They are fighting for worship in the courts of Mammon. The garden is no longer given. We have got to choose. We can renounce the claim to be makers, and then we refuse our destiny as men; we can cultivate our own garden in seclusion and ignore the world, and then we refuse our destiny as members of a family; we can try to separate making from worship, and then we renounce our wholeness. Or we can labor to remake not our own private garden merely but the garden of humanity to the glory of God; and then we fulfil our destiny in its fullness.

But we cannot renounce the birthright of making unless we renounce also the birthright of love, for love impels us to make. And similarly we cannot lead the world back to making unless we first lead it back to love. The love-song is the epitome of all art. The artist and the lover sing because of the beauty of what they see; the saint sings—and his song reaches to the ends of the earth, to the miserable and the outcast, to the least of God's creatures—because he has seen the Beauty that embraces all beauty, and his soul is filled with the Love that embraces all love, and his whole life and every moment of it are not only the making of beauty and the making of worship but the remaking of the world, because he cannot rest until he has brought the whole of creation back with him in unity of song and worship, to mirror once more the beauty and the creative love of God.

VI

The Making of the Family

We are not real men and women unless we are both lovers and makers, and unless our making is the expression of our love. The primary form of making, therefore, is the making of love. For there you have the two things, the overcoming of isolation, the joy of making, in one. Love-making both presupposes the state of living in love and at the same time perfects it: you cannot overcome your isolation completely in a day. In the ordinary way, men and women are incomplete without the fulfilment of body, mind and heart which love of one another brings them. They are incomplete without the fulfilment which transfigures the flesh and gives it a beauty which age cannot destroy. They are incomplete without the fulfilment which comes of the marriage of true minds: the minds of man and woman work normally in different ways, so that each is completed in the other. They are incomplete without the fulfilment of the heart and will, for it is only when these are made whole by the shared life of love that the union in flesh and mind becomes a making of love.

It is a lifelong process. That is one reason why marriage in itself, and not because of any arbitrary law of God or man, should be indissoluble. If you think that love-making is a pleasant occupation for a passing moment and no more, you will flit over the surface of life; you will never be a lover, because you will never be fully alive. It is a thing that takes a lifetime to complete. It is also a thing that can only be done by man and woman together. That is why you have to be so gentle when you are making love.

You have to find not separate pleasure but real oneness through the bodily union. So many marriages are wrecked or made unhappy because of a blindness at the beginning about the danger of relapsing into isolation in the moments of passion, or perhaps even because of total ignorance of the shock which the first revelation of passion itself may produce. It is easy to let passion make you greedy and, therefore, brutal; but even though you are gentle in soul, you may still do irreparable damage if you lack knowledge; if you allow the brutality of an abrupt disclosure where there should be the gradual discovery in common of a common joy.

The pride and greed and brutality of passion may frighten and horrify; to have known much beforehand in theory will not necessarily prepare for the realization of knowledge in lived experience. When you are making love, it is not body making love to body, but man and woman making love to one another; if the mind is hurt it may well kill desire in the body; if the body is hurt it may well turn love into hatred. When you begin to make love, you are concerned not with a biological function but with a human mystery, with human love; it may be necessary to spend much time, perhaps whole days, in preparing the body and the whole being gradually for the final union, so that it may become something for which the whole being longs as for an inevitable climax and completion, and not something thrust on it suddenly and frighteningly from without.

And not only at the beginning but always there is the same need for gentleness and reverence; because a caress which is not the fulfilment of the common desire of both is not a caress but a plundering. No two people are exactly alike in intensity of passion; that is why the achievement of real union in bodily love-making is not a thing that is done in a day. But even if you have that, still there is always the same need to prepare the whole being for the consummation of bodily love, to progress together in order to reach it together, and then not to regard this moment of life as concluded until body and mind alike are soothed and fulfilled and at peace.

It is terrible when young people are left in ignorance of these things. But nowadays there is an opposite danger. If you think, as some people would have us think, that a knowledge of the technique of bodily love-making is sufficient you will still miss the meaning of love-making. Those books which set out to supply this information may be useful or even necessary; but the safe thing is to have learnt sufficiently well to be able to afford to forget, as far as conscious deliberation is concerned. Otherwise you will be in danger of a cerebral concentration on physical dexterity, and then you will sink into isolation again, and you will forget that, when you make love, you fulfil more than the desire of the flesh. Love is also the marriage of true minds. This is not a body but a woman, and so I must worship; this is not a body but a man, and so I must comfort and protect him in my arms. Love-making is not only, it is not even primarily, the gift of the body's rapture; it is the lifelong labor of becoming one mind and one heart. That is achieved in part through the body; but it is achieved through every moment and every aspect of the common life; it is achieved through the work and play, the variety of interests, the thinking and planning, the constant gradual growth of character and temperament to maturity, that make up the life of every day.

115

It is achieved by, as well as expressed in, the making of the family. Just as the artist is not complete until the vision, which makes him one with the reality seen and loved, is expressed in stone or words or music, so the lovers are not complete until their love is bodied forth in a third person, and the image of the Trinity is fulfilled. The childless love is incomplete, just as the man without art is incomplete.

People sometimes criticize the practice of contraception on the grounds that it is a selfish snatching at a pleasure torn from its human context, and that it makes love uncreative. Neither of these arguments is exact. The first may be true of some cases; it is untrue of others where the physical union is the expression of deep love. The second is inaccurate because all real love-making is creative: the lovers make their own love and unity.

What is true is that contraception tears love-making from its human completeness, and destroys a great part—the perfection—of its creativeness. The childless marriage can indeed be a creative thing; but the willfully childless marriage is of itself turned away from creativeness. The same is true of every act of physical union. Love is always outward-turning, always an impulsion to making; and if you willfully frustrate it and turn it in upon itself, it becomes destructive and may well in the end become self-destructive. Some people find that contraception kills love-making itself, because it kills spontaneity and introduces an atmosphere of chilly calculation. They could argue with equal force philosophically: to make barren what is of its nature creative is a monstrosity. They could argue with still greater force theologically: if you thus frustrate the completeness of love-making, you are taking the power whereby you become the "ministers of God's omnipotence" in the making of an immortal child, who in its turn is called to share God's own life, and you are turning that power directly away from its purpose.

You are right to control the size of the family: the optimum is certainly not necessarily the maximum; and you have to decide by considering two possibly opposing good things: the glory of making with God immortal children who shall see God, and the necessity of providing the sort of life for them that will best help them to learn to see God. But you can do all this without destroying anything.

Still, suppose two people who really and deeply love one another but who just cannot afford to marry and have children: are they to be made unhappy for the rest of their lives by the tragic absurdity of an economic system? (And what a light it throws on our modern world, that civilized people should be robbed of rights which the most primitive savage enjoys as a matter of course.) It is intolerably hard; but we should not blame Christian morality for the hardship. The thing is not wrong because it is forbidden; it is forbidden because it is wrong. And when we are tempted to think of a refusal to compromise in cases like this as an injustice, it is perhaps because we look only at one aspect of the thing. We may treat men and women with all the reverence they demand, but we forget that sex in man is also to be treated like that; we forget that it is not just a physical event which we can treat simply as such; we tend to isolate one aspect of it—its power to express love—from its wholeness. (We do the same with other things, too: think how, if you are being unjust, you can blind yourself to your victim's point of view if the injustice benefits somebody else whom you love.) And so we fail to reverence the material of this making; and we go back to the world of the men of power, and refuse the gift of wholeness.

Love is both made and expressed in the making of the family. The child is the parents' love made flesh; and at the same time, in the making of the child, they make their own oneness. In the birth of the child, they are completed; but the new life in which they now live, the human trinity, has its own laws. Every human being is unique. What a tragedy it is when a child has to grow up without the constant loving presence of father and mother—yet there are some people who regard it as such a good thing that they would have all children brought up in common by the State. If it is a crime to regiment men and women, it is a worse crime to regiment children. How will they ever learn to live in love when they have never for a moment been allowed to know the life of love? They will have all the benefits of modern science and modern hygiene; but who will cherish their souls? There are some things no stranger will ever understand, however kind and gentle; there are some things that only the mother understands, because she understands not with her mind only but with her body. Do you think there can be much hope for a world in which families are all the time being broken up, children all the time having to abandon home and mother or father for a new home and a new mother or father? Do you think there can be any wisdom where there is no tranquility, where the life-work of love-making is never completed, where even the idea of the gradual discovery of a shared wholeness is forgotten? Impermanence and shallowness increase together. A lifelong permanence is needed for man and woman to make their love; but how much more the children need it.

But there are cases where all this does not apply, where the marriage is a failure and the home a hell? Yes, there are. But that cannot mean that the nature of things in themselves can

118

be changed. A positive law can be abrogated or dispensed; but moral truths are not positive laws: the things they forbid are not wrong because somebody says so, they are wrong because they destroy the nature of things. The law of gravitation can be a very cruel law on occasion; but it is no use saying that it ought to be abrogated. Things go wrong because there is evil in the world; but that is no excuse for making yet greater disorder. When things go wrong, they cause great pain and suffering: Christian hope consists not in trying to pretend for a time that the nature of things can be changed, that black can be white, but that God can and does use the suffering we cause in order to lead us to discover reality and to learn how to love and to be worth loving.

Love-making is the making of the family. Think of the family as the complete thing: the home and all who live in it.

The home itself; for the home is, again, the extension of the personality, made by the man and woman and in its turn helping to make them. What a lot those people miss who have their homes made and furnished for them by a firm without even knowing what the result will be like. Perhaps it helps explain the chilly impersonality of so many lives. Your home should be like your clothes and your conversation: a part of yourself. Have an artist to design for you if you will, but see that he makes something that you can make your own.

And those who live in the home: how unwise and un-Christian we are if we think of the family as just the parents and the children in a house where there are others besides these. If you have a large household with a number of small children, you will need help; and what could be more valuable or more dignified for a girl than to learn in a family which is living in love the art of making a home of her own? But no; our forefathers may have abolished serfdom; but they continued to talk about servants; they relegated them to dark underground rooms during the day and icy attics for the night, and treated them as though they belonged to an inferior species; and now some people are surprised that there is what is called a domestic service problem. The Christian family, at any rate, ought to be very different. There is diversity of gifts but the same Spirit. Father, mother, children, those who help: they have each a different office to perform, but together they make the home. We are made by what we make. The parents make the children, teach them to grow to maturity; but they learn more than they teach. They give orders; but their authority, unless they are very blind, will teach them to obey.

The making of the child is not completed until the child is ready to become a man and a citizen. But the child is always this unique child and not another. Between the small family which is the home and the large family which is human society, there comes the school.

Some people think of school as a necessary evil, necessary because parents have neither time nor ability to give their children all the information they will need for life in the world. But that is of secondary importance. Citizenship is an art, demanding apprenticeship and practice. You have to learn two things simultaneously: to see and treat humanity as a family, and to be strong and independent and undaunted in face of opposition or hostility. The life of the home prepares for these things; but to begin to practice them you need a larger, a less closely knit society. To acquire a virtue you must have experience of the material of the virtue.

But at the same time, if the school is to teach you to see humanity as a family, it must be itself a family: it must be an extension of the home. Send your child to one of those vast establishments where he will of necessity become little more than a number, where he will be regimented to a pattern, and left to get what he can out of a common discipline: he will certainly not learn thereby to see humanity as a family, he will learn to think of mastery in the world in terms of subjecting others to the same sort of discipline, to subordinate personality to regimented tidiness, and to judge, as he was judged, by externals. It will never occur to him that life in the world should be, like life in the home, the making of a family. He may learn to be an obedient economic or political unit; he may also learn to be an efficient administrator or a man of power; he will not learn to be a lover and maker. The school, if it is not to do more harm than good, must be an extension of the home: the first thing necessary is a family atmosphere, and the idea that children and teachers are there to join together in making the school a home.

You go to school to learn; but school should teach you primarily to see and to make. Important to know many facts: you cannot do without them. But what a tragedy when the accumulation of this knowledge stifles and kills the power to see and love and make. The young child loves to draw and paint, and the drawings and paintings are lovely; why is education in England allowed to kill all this? It is natural that this creative love should turn after a time to other modes of expression; it is monstrous that it should be entirely quenched. There is no reason why all the things that are taught in school should not be made to serve vision and art instead of destroying them. Mathematics can give you a sense of order and structure; history can show you, not an assemblage of dead facts, but the still living, still unfinished human story in which you yourself are vitally involved; geography can show you what other branches of the human family are

121

like and how they live their lives. These firings are information, but they can teach you to see and help you to make. But above all these in importance is the introduction to the art and to the poetry, whether in prose or in verse, of our own and other races: for this is not information but immediate vision; and though the ridiculous demands of examining bodies try to turn it into a study of historical data and allusions and textual problems and irrelevant facts about the lives of authors, it is none of these things, but an immediate awareness of the reality expressed, an immediate sharing also of a living tradition in which, again, you yourself are vitally involved, and which you have to take up and add to and pass on.

But if we simply try to impose and compel knowledge, we may well do more harm than good. Drudgery there must be, here as elsewhere, and the need of discipline; but there is no reason why we should not at least try to encourage the child to teach himself. If we see something and find it lovely, we want to know it better. If study springs from vision and serves its demands, it becomes not a dreary discipline but an endless voyage of discovery: not a passive and unwilling receiving but a process of making.

The child's power of vision must be cherished, enlarged, deepened: to destroy it is a sort of murder. But the child has to learn also to be a man, a master and maker; and there is nothing to which this does not apply. Information must be the servant of vision; it must also be accompanied by a growth in the power of criticism, a growth in that form of making which we call the art of thought. What is the good of teaching the young to read if their ability to read will only lay them open to the influence of propaganda? Reading is dangerous without discrimination. You have to help them to make their own minds, to form the power of judging for themselves; only so can you train them for freedom.

Discipline, again, is drab and sterile if it is founded simply on fear of punishment; that way you produce not human beings but mindless automata; you will not even produce obedience, for only a free man can obey—a machine can only conform to external pressure. But they need to learn more than to obey: they need to learn to rule; and they need to learn to rule, not as men of power, but as members of a family. So you must have discipline, for if you abolish it, you will produce only spineless selfishness; but you must show that discipline is a creative thing, the scaffolding on which this home is built; and you must help the young to help in the making of it, showing them the reason for rules, inviting discussion of them, training them to preserve the order of the family life, or, when necessary, to help in the changing of it freely and responsibly, and as they grow up giving them a more active share in authority. But you must train them to rule not a regiment but a family; train them to realize gradually that every human being is unique and must be reverenced, that discipline, if it is to be human, must be tempered with humor, and that order, if it is to be creative, must be motivated by love.

And always you have to remember that it is not just a mind or a character that you are dealing with: it is a human being. Body, mind, character, all need training if they are to be healthy; but you cannot train them independently of one another. If you train the body and ignore the mind, you will destroy the human being, and ultimately the body, too. If you force the mind's development and ignore the body, you will frustrate the life of the mind itself. If you attempt to form the character as though it had nothing to do with the life of the mind, with the power to see and to think and criticize, you will be likely to produce only a split personality, in which character is no more than a number of conditioned reflexes bearing little relation to the moral life of man. The growth that you have to consider is the growth of the whole personality. Sport is good for the body; but if you turn it into a fetish, it is bad for the human being; if it is so completely organized that it kills initiative, it is bad for the human being; if it is brutalizing to the mind, it is bad; if instead of developing the family spirit, it plays down to the herd instinct, it is bad. So with study. It can be forced; it can be unreal; it can be uncreative; it can be uncritical; or it can ignore or frustrate the rest of the human being: and then it is bad. So with a moral training which consists in a number of disjointed negative precepts; which attempts to shackle the mind or repress the instincts and emotions instead of helping them to develop to wholeness: it is bad. The human being cannot grow in an atmosphere of emotional repression: the prudery which attempts to suppress the emotional life of the child through the natural stages of development or to safeguard a negative innocence by the cult of ignorance is bound to have disastrous effects, to stunt the life of the mind and the growth of character as well.

We cannot overstress the importance of trying as far as possible to substitute the interest that leads the child to teach itself for the force or fear that will cram knowledge into it; nor can we overstress the importance of the relationship between pupils and teacher and between the pupils themselves—in the first case, we must at least have sympathy and emotional harmony, in the second we must have, not the cut-throat competition which turns them into men of power, but the realization that they are all engaged together in the making of a common life and work.

124

The Making of the Family

To help the growing child to enlarge and deepen its vision and therefore its love, and at the same time to help it to become a maker—maker of its own life as a whole human being with body, mind, heart and will, and of its home, and of the larger family of the school, and eventually of the world-family: that is the aim of education. And we might add that if, in trying to educate the young, we fail to teach them that education is something that is never finished this side the grave, we have failed altogether. If we try to educate in freedom, we shall have many bitter disappointments, and sometimes we shall be tempted to despair; but God has daily His far more dreadful disappointments, and He does not despair.

The growth of body, mind, heart and will can only be a true growth if it is the growth of the whole human being. But still the end will be chaos unless the growth of the human being is gathered up into a constant act of worship. It is something to keep safe the power of vision; but to see the manifold in wholeness and oneness, you must learn to see it in the One. But the individual is not alone. It is the family that grows; and it is the family that worships, for the worship is the substance of the growth. The fine old tradition of family prayers should be revived; when it is not allowed to become an empty external ritual but is really a common prayer, really a gathering of the family in God, it can do immense things. It takes the common life of love to God to be blessed and made holy; it is the offering, not of the individuals merely, but of the individuals in their wholeness, in their first and most precious environment; and so the blessing that will come to them is a blessing on their unity. Where there is this common life of worship—and what applies to the home should apply to the school, and the actual prayer should not be divided from, but expressed in, the whole of the daily life—there cannot be a relapse into isolation; there cannot be the grasping selfishness that kills the life of love; you are learning to live life fully because you are learning that there are better reasons for loving and helping and serving than the profit motive, and so you are learning to see the greater world as a family. That is why a society in which family life is decaying is itself inevitably a decaying society: you will have only an aggregate of State-controlled individuals instead of the happiness of a shared life and purpose. You learn in the family to make the common life of love: you learn that it is not a thing that you can do alone. But when you have done this you are not at the end, you are at the beginning. Love is always outward-turning; and as the love of man and woman is made by, as well as expressed in, the making of the family, so the love of the family is made by and expressed in the making of the world. If you love in God you will be saved from exclusiveness; and the closer you come to Him the wider your love will spread. If you can say implicitly of every action, "I am doing this because I love the family and because in the family I love God," you will bring to the family an ever-increasing depth and intensity of life and power, and the power will more and more go out from you, and enchant and help and console the world.

But always the wicket swings. You cannot learn to make this full and complex life without suffering disappointments and setbacks. There will be times when the tension of living many lives in one will wear you down. There will be tension between your selfishness and your love; there will be tension between the love of man and woman and their common love of the family; there will be tension between either or both of these and the demands of the world; and always the wicket swings and human love is in danger of rivalling God. You can

126

become wrapped up in your human happiness and forget your need of God; or you will find at times that your human love wants to be its own master and challenge the will of God—you will be in danger of the primal sin. You cannot live a life that is worth living and expect it always to be smooth and neat. But it is just for these difficulties that a special sacrament is given us. If you expect the life of love to be endless ecstasy, or the building of the family an endless and effortless joy, you will be sadly disillusioned. But if you accept drudgery and difficulties and tensions as well as joy as the stuff of life and the stuff of worship, then you will, in fact, be making a happiness that will come to you, now and hereafter, without your seeking and beyond your desiring, The Book of Tobias gently teaches us that gentleness and worship are the conditions of the life of love: Tobias and Sara first learn to pray together, and only then, when they are sure that their life will be lived in God, are they "in their own wedlock."

"Unless the Lord build the house, they labor in vain that build it." If in spite of the difficulties and perhaps the apparent contradictions you are faithful, and build always in the love and the power of God, you will build an eternal beatitude. You will build, not in the shifting sands of selfishness, but on imperishable rock. You will build a beatitude beyond your knowledge or your dreams; for your own love will shed its light and warmth in an ever-widening circle upon the world, and perhaps you will not know till the end how many have thought of your house as home, how many have been led by the sight of your love and your happiness to discover their infinite Source. But in the end you will know, and your joy will be filled; for all the trials and labors of life will seem a very small price to have paid when you meet in eternity these other children whom you have brought there, and when you take them, still your children, by the hand, and lead them to the breathless wonder of God's presence, the inexhaustible happiness of the everlasting home.

VII

The Making of the World

Our Lord said to the Jews, "You shall know the truth, and the truth shall make you free." St. Paul said to the Galatians: "Stand, and be not holden in again with the yoke of servitude." All down the ages you hear the cry of the oppressed praying for freedom; the call of freedom has always been able to rally men to fight and if necessary to die. But what is freedom? It is possible to follow a battle-cry only to find it an ambiguity; to fight for a cause and find at the end that it is the wrong cause.

The truth shall make you free. We fear the tyranny of external events, of disease and disaster and death; and to some extent we can overcome the fear by overcoming the power of nature to hurt us: we can overcome disease, we can avert some of the catastrophes which nature brings upon us; but we cannot avert them all, and we cannot escape death. But the truth can make us free: for if we live in wholeness and know already the life of eternity, death and disaster will not dismay us, because we shall know that they cannot alter the substance of our being. We want to be free of the tyranny of men; but can we wholly escape this either? For just as man is part of the universe, and compared with the might and immensity of the universe is a puny speck of unimaginable smallness, so too in a smaller compass he is part of human society, a "social animal" standing in need of society's help for his own economic, political, cultural life, but largely at the mercy of the herd, and at least bound his life within it by the bondage of the law. Even if he is free of the domination of a foreign people, how can he be wholly free? Only the truth can make him free.

St. Paul wrote, "We are not under the law but under grace"; but he wrote also, "I was not without the law of God, but was in the law of Christ." And St. Augustine tells us that it is one thing to be under the law and another to be in the law; for "whoso is in the law acteth according to the law; whoso is under the law is acted upon according to the law." Freedom and authority seem to be in contradiction; but they need not be so. Was Christ the less free because He could not sin?

There is a freedom which is the opposite of slavery; we can have this freedom and still not be free. There is a freedom from the bondage of sin, for sin makes man not his own master but the slave of his vices; we can have this inner freedom and still not be wholly free. There is the further freedom which Christ promises us, the freedom from the bondage of the law; and this freedom we cannot find by abolishing the law as we try to abolish disease, for so we should only sink back into the worse, the less than human, bondage of sin; we can find it only by finding the truth, not as something external to us, but in ourselves, not as something we can gain possession of, but as something which, if we are humble, will take possession of us.

When Socrates said that sin is ignorance he was right, but not wholly right. We can possess the truth and still do wrong, for evil is in the will; but we cannot be wholly possessed by the truth and still do wrong, for when truth takes possession of us, it takes possession of the whole being, we cannot store it away in an intellectual vacuum, we become one with it in mind and will alike.

And are we then free? Yes, we are free with the freedom of the lover. Christ's inability to sin is the summit of His freedom; being wholly possessed by truth, He stood in no danger of falling under the bondage of sin, for sin was wholly alien to Him, and He stood in no danger of falling under the bondage of the law, for His will and the law were one. To obey because we are forced is bondage; to obey because we love and, therefore, will to obey is freedom. Christ said, "The truth shall make you free"; but He *is* the truth: if we are one with Christ to the point of being able to say, "it is Thyself," we shall do the will of Christ, but we shall be free as the wind that bloweth where it listeth, for our desires and His desires will be one.

But there will still be the constraints imposed by human society: and can these leave us free? Yes, they can; though they may not. They can, if their purpose is what it ought to be—to make possible the living of a full and happy life for all the human beings who make up the society; and also if we for our part are possessed by the truth, for then the good of society will be our own good, we shall be whole and happy in so far as we can serve. "Whereas I was free of all," St. Paul says again, "I made myself the servant of all." Truth makes us free, but love makes us willing servants. Every human being is unique, and has a sort of infinity about him; every human being has a divine destiny, and society exists to serve it. On the other hand, every human being is a part of human society, and must serve society. There seems to be an insoluble contradiction, but there is not; for the divine destiny is to love, and love means the will to serve. If we think of the two things as separate we shall think them contradictory; on the one side, we shall have selfishness preying on society, on the other, we shall have tyranny degrading men and women. But if we know what it means to be possessed by the truth, we shall know what love means; and then we shall not keep the two things separate, we shall, of necessity, put them together; and we shall have neither selfishness nor tyranny, but a family.

There will always be tension; there will always be the temptation, even when society is justly ordered, to spoil the wholeness of man in his environment. We can overstate the duty of service, and then we turn service into servitude; we can overstress the right of freedom, and turn freedom into selfishness and license. Just because we cannot adequately serve society as robots or half-men, we have rights which society will not touch if it values its life, quite apart from the fact that because we are greater than the world it *may* not touch them. The right to live, the right to think our own thoughts, to follow our own conscience, to worship God, the right to found a family, the right to fulfil our own vocation by choosing for ourselves what form of making our life-work shall be—all these rights are ours just because we are human beings and not slaves either to a State or to a machine; but unless these rights are respected society will suffer as well as the individual.

For this family too, like the smaller family of the home, is something that has to be made, and can only be made by the common love and labors of all its members. How will you contribute if you have no mind of your own, no initiative, no judgment, and if the power of making is itself stunted by a tyranny that takes away your art? A family is not a dead thing, made, finished and thenceforward unchanging: it is a life, and life is movement. Society has its structure, its laws; but these are only one aspect of it. On the other side, there is the constant change of circumstance: new discoveries, new powers, new opportunities, produce new need of adjustment; so that the mind and temperament of man in society is never still. And therefore, when we leave the realm of what is called natural law—the pattern of life itself—and come down to positive human laws and conventions, there is always a tension between the existing order and its need of renewal.

In practice, indeed, the social structure tends to lag behind the movement of life, and so to fail to fulfil its requirements: first, because too often the power to make change rests with those who have grown accustomed to an established order and fail to see its inability to meet the demands of new life; second, because the vested interests fear lest any change should diminish their power or importance; third, because the need of safeguarding order and security frequently degenerates into the imposition of uniformity, into standardization, and standardization is the destruction of life and initiative. You find historically that the innovators, however beneficial and even urgently necessary their reforms, are usually treated with suspicion and faced with endless obstacles; so that there is nearly always, at any given moment of a society's life, a tension between those who realize the new needs and those who from ignorance or malice oppose them. (There is the further tension between those who work for a new way which will really benefit mankind and those who merely seek to destroy, or to set up a new way which is evil or mistaken.)

But always the emergence of the new forms depends on the men and women who make up society. There will be outstanding personalities, no doubt, who will lead the new age, but everybody is involved; it is not only, or even primarily, the politicians who make political life: it is the artists and writers, the makers of music, it is all men of vision, who make the "new spirit"; and the struggle between the old

133

order and the new will be decided not least by the infinitely complex interplay of the lives and personalities of ordinary men and women. We must be real men and women if we want to make a real contribution to the building of society; but if we are, in fact, real men and women, we shall, in fact, fight on the side of life against decay and death, even though we are unconscious of fighting at all.

The constraints of society will not leave you free if they are totally unjust; they will not leave you free if they represent an order which has ceased to correspond to the needs of life; but as long as you remain free to fight against them, you can still be free despite the tension within you, for to fight for your family is itself an act of freedom because it is an affirmation of your own life. To serve society adequately, you need to be a whole man; but to be a whole man, you need to serve society. Suppose a social order which worked tolerably well in an immature state of society, where the masses could only be content if they were to a large extent dependent on and led by a small minority; and suppose that the old order lingers on long after the masses have achieved independence of mind and the ability, and hence the desire, to make their own lives and to play a part in making the life of society, you would have an order which had become unjust by reason of its inability to meet the needs of the new life, and you would have to try to change it. Its continuance would fetter you intolerably; but none the less, your fighting would itself be a freedom: the overcoming of obstacles would give you fortitude, the virtue of the martyrs—and who more than the martyrs who laugh at death are free? But then this is to talk only of inward freedom, for the martyr is certainly not externally free? No, it is both inward and external freedom—the martyr would not come down from his cross if he could. He wants to be where he is; and he wants to be where he is because he wants to serve his family. He is indeed the supreme example of the man who fights for the new spirit, the new way, and in fighting, yes, and in dying, is fully free— free because what he does he does of his own free will, and fully free because, by doing what he does, he is made whole.

We make ourselves by making our family. Even a social order which is just will put constraints upon us, just as the life of the home puts constraints upon us; but that need not destroy our freedom. Often there will be real conflicts of duties in practice, conflicts between my own needs and the needs of my family and the needs of society; for real life is seldom tidy. Often the thing will be complicated by the fact that the common good of society is not a stable thing: it will put far greater demands on me in times of crisis than in times of tranquility. But the fact that the common life interferes with my own desires at surface level does not mean that it interferes with my freedom; for it is when I am selfish that I am not free.

We in this country have seen all too clearly the effects of an interpretation of freedom which makes it synonymous with the absence of all duties to society; and the terrible effects of free competition and untrammelled selfishness have produced a vehement desire for justice expressed in the demand for a planned society. And if we have a planned society, must we lose our freedom? Shall we find ourselves led into the worse evil of a political control of every moment and every aspect of our lives in the name of the common good? Shall we find that for the false god of the self we have only substituted the equally false god of the State? There is no reason why it should be so, unless we are very stupid. There are our natural rights, without which we cannot be men and

women at all: if we lose these we lose everything, for ourselves and for society as well. But apart from these? We shall
have to revise our ideas about many things; we shall find that
in many ways perhaps we must have less in order that others
may have more; some of the things we have come to think of
as rights and liberties will have to be forgone. But if all this is
necessary precisely for justice? We have to choose: either we
want a just social order, and then we implicitly want those
things which will make it just, so that in acting in accordance
with them we fulfil our own will and are free; or we want the
continuance of old injustice, we want to keep our own
regardless of the needs of the family, and then we implicitly
refuse the wholeness that comes to us only from living in the
family, and, being at the mercy of the autonomous false self,
we cease to be free.

We have a right to live our own lives and to found a family;
and that implies the right to make the future of the home as
stable and secure as is humanly possible: it implies the right
to some form of property. But that does not mean that we
can ever be absolute owners of anything. We are only stewards for God. Legally a man may do what he likes with his
own; but not morally. Morally you may not use your possessions in a way that will hurt the common good of society;
you may not cling to them selfishly while others starve; you
may not waste them; you may not acquiesce in gross inequalities of wealth: for if you are miserly or irresponsible, you
follow the false self. You have a right to property in order to
be able to live a dignified human life with your family and to
make your own home; but that does not mean necessarily
that it must be private property in the sense that no one else
has a share in it, and it cannot mean that no one else has a
right to share in it even if the alternative is starvation. Every

right implies a corresponding duty: the more you have from society the more you must serve society. That is simple justice; though, if you are wise, you will try to go beyond justice to charity and give society the willing service of love, for then you will be free.

"If a man will not work, neither let him eat," said St. Paul. To be a whole man, you need society; but to be a whole man, you need also to serve society. There is no place in a human social order for the man who sets out simply to get rich himself at the expense of his fellow-men. Is the profit motive evil then? Not at all; but a social order based exclusively on the profit motive is evil. A social order in which the profit motive is not regulated by the common needs of society is evil. To say that we are all involved in the making of society is to say that we have each of us a special function to fulfil: we choose our own form of making according to our own particular gifts and desires, but it is more than a purely personal thing, it is something we contribute to the life of the human family. It is right that those who give more should receive more, but it is *only* right because they give more; there are inequalities of function because (outside the great natural rights and the supreme common destiny, where all men are equal) there are inequalities of gifts; and, therefore, there can be inequalities in the reward given for the duties performed. But the idea that a man has an absolute right to whatever he can make is an evil idea. You can justify profits, but only as a particular form of wages for work done; you can justify interest, but only as a form of compensation for risks taken. The Church has always condemned usury; and it is not simply exorbitant rates of interest that are condemned, but usury in itself: what nowadays is called "pure interest," a payment on a loan, fixed beforehand, and without risk to the lender. The essence of usury, as Tawney points out, is that it is certain, and that whether the borrower gains or loses, the usurer takes his pound of flesh.[1]

The profit motive unchecked by social responsibility is only one of the innumerable ways in which the self-assertive instinct finds an outlet at the expense of the common life. That instinct is not evil in itself; it is evil when it kills the common life; and what we have to do is to harness it, like all our other energies, to the service of the family as well as ourselves. You can assert yourself against society; you can equally well assert yourself for society; but to do it you need a clear vision of the end in view and a strong enough motive to override the demands of the false self. You need charity.

Perhaps that is one of the strongest reasons why the making of the human family should be the work of relatively small groups. Just as you cannot expect to find the atmosphere of home in a school so large that the children cease to be regarded as human beings and become mere units, so you cannot expect the idea of community to flourish in a society which consists simply in a single centralized authority and a vast amorphous mass of individuals. You have a much better example of a reasonable human order in the little village school where the children learn to be a family, so as later on to make their lives together in the village as a village community. If you want an order which is alive and not a dead standardization, you must start from the small unit and go by gradual stages to the large: the individual man and woman finding their life in their home; the home helping to make the life of the village or town; this in its turn helping to form the

[1] R. H. Tawney: *Religion and the Rise of Capitalism*, Penguin edition, 54.

life of the larger community of district or county or province; and only then coming, through the various contributions of these parts of the nation, to the life of the nation itself, which in its turn has its part to play, its particular gift to bring to the life of the world.

As modern transport and communications knit the world more closely together, you need a corresponding evolution in the centralization of authority; but if this is done at the expense of the life of the small groups, you will kill the society you are trying to preserve. When national sovereignty absorbs all power into itself, as it has, in fact, been doing, it does a double wrong to humanity: by clinging to complete autonomy it leaves the world a prey to national aggressiveness—it is Hobbes's state of nature on an international scale; and by taking away the partial independence of the smaller groups it gradually destroys the wholeness of life of their members.

In politics as in industry, if you can really share with others the making of a life and the mastery of its material, you can really serve: and you are more likely to want to serve, for you will be able to see that in helping the community, you are helping your own life. What a sub-human slavery it is when vast industrial organizations are owned and controlled by a few, and the masses are reduced to giving their lives to labor which is uncreative in itself and uncreative also because they have no control over the way the work is done! If you want a human society, you must use mechanical invention in such a way as to help man's power of making instead of taking it from him; and you must so organize industry that all have some share in the ownership and the control—which probably means that you must organize it into smaller units, and with electrical power there is no reason why you should not be able to do so. Then, perhaps, you will remedy the frightful state of affairs in which work, for the mass of men and women, is no more than a drudgery, and a drudgery which is entirely their own private affair: you may recover alike the creativeness and the sense of social responsibility which is still to be found in some of the professions, where beyond the profit motive there is a deep feeling of vocation: the feeling of the value of making in itself, and of the value and dignity of making for the common good of society. And the same is true of what are called the social services, though they can too easily become not a service at all but the tyranny of a fussy bureaucratic interference: you have to see that they always respect the great natural rights; you have to make sure that they are not an attempt to dragoon people, but an assurance to them of opportunity to enjoy the advantages which a modern society can provide, and ought as a matter of course to provide, for its citizens.

We have seen enough and to spare of the evil which robs men of their manhood and turns them into mindless automata whose only life is the life of the State. Perhaps we are not so much on our guard against other, more insidious, ways in which we may lose our manhood. Political society is the union of many families working together for a common end; and because an orderly working together implies authority, it implies the State which is the subject of that authority. But the State is thus by definition limited in its authority: it is limited primarily by the law of God, the moral law; but it is limited also by the fact that its purpose is to secure the happiness of society, and society means men and women. There is more in this than merely the respecting of the natural rights of man. We in this country pride ourselves on being a democracy; but we should remember what democracy means. In an autocratic régime the king can truthfully say, "I am the State," for all power is vested in him; in a democracy it is every individual who has to say, "I am the State," for the meaning of democracy is that all work together and all have power to make society. We are each responsible for all.

If, then, you allow those who for the moment have power in your name to dictate to you and turn you into a machine, you resign your democratic heritage: if Nelson had said, not England expects, but England compels every man to do his duty, it would have been impossible for any man to do his duty. You resign your human heritage also: for you resign your mind and will, and you resign your hope of restoration—we hope and fight for the restoration of human beings, not for the restoration of a shopful of machines.

But you lose your heritage also if you allow the State to take away your initiative, not in the name of its own exclusive right to power and glory, but in the name of your own well-being. The State can kill by kindness. It *will* kill by kindness if you allow it to turn society into a kindergarten. If you allow it to become something outside society, something to which you are passive, instead of remembering that it is only a group of people who are supposed to hold power in your name and at your pleasure; if you allow it to do for you things which it is part of your human life of making to do for yourself, then you lose your heritage, even though you lose it so gradually that you fail to notice your loss. The first stage is to sink into selfishness and forget the ideal of a common work; that stage we know, and we have found that it takes a major war to shake us out of it and recover the sense of a common purpose. (That fact is not a justification for war; it is only an exposure of what is called peace.) The second stage follows inevitably: you treat it as a matter of course that the

State should take over from you the work, not only of building society, but even of the making of your own life. You will be killed, not by State tyranny, but by social service.

The grouping of many families constitutes the city, the grouping of many cities constitutes the nation; the grouping of many nations ought to constitute the world-society. Science has made the world a unity; nationalism breaks it up again into warring fragments. Internationally, we are still at the stage when every individual is for himself, and there is no central authority to keep justice and peace, and life is "nasty, brutish and short." You can trace the source of the trouble to the breakdown of the unity of Christendom in the sixteenth century if you will: the trouble was not the emergence of national societies, but the emergence of nationalist societies. Nations are like individuals: they have their own natural rights, the right to make their own lives in independence, the right to their own ways of life, their own culture and institutions; but again, every right implies a corresponding duty; they cannot claim these rights in defiance of the common good of the world; on the contrary, as each nation has its own peculiar gifts, so it has its own peculiar function to perform, its own particular gift to bring to the community of nations. Like the individual, it must have a sense of vocation: a vocation to serve the world.

It has to acknowledge the claims of justice: justice towards other nations, as in the respecting of treaties; justice towards the common good, as in the substitution of cooperation for cutthroat competition. But if the nation is living in wholeness, it will go further than this, as charity goes further than justice: it will be ready not only to respect the rights of others but even to sacrifice its own if by so doing it can help others. M. Maritain once said that perhaps the world would have

142

to wait for a Christ-nation, a nation which would sacrifice itself on the cross for the sake of the whole world, that the whole world might be won back from the isolation and enmities of the false self, and become a family...

Peace, at any rate, is the result of charity, not of justice. Justice removes the impediments to peace; but you must have more than that. You must have the will to help in building the world at the cost of self-sacrifice; and only charity can give you that. What is the use of making blueprints for a new society when the will to build is lacking, when behind the blueprints there lurks the old spirit of selfishness and competition? You cannot live for the common good of the nations unless you can see the nations as a single family and will to treat them as a single family; and for that you must have the vision of the oneness of the world, the oneness of the world in God. You must have organization and law, and sufficient power vested in a central authority to ensure that the law is preserved—which means that you must have a measure of abrogation of national sovereignty; but again you must have the will to alter the structure of this international society as the needs of its members change; and all the time, throughout this double movement of the making of law and the changing of law, you will need the charity which can see beyond the immediate selfish profit-motive of the nation, and which realizes that the nation, like the individual, becomes fully itself only in the wider environment of the life of the human family.

Certainly, goodwill alone is not enough. Just as, to make your own life, you need a keen judgment and a level head and plenty of hard thinking, and just as, in the life of the home, you are helpless unless, as well as love, you have the ability to think out your problems and make decisions and plan with prudence for the future: so in national and international life also. That is why in economics we need the expert, in politics we need the statesman; and those of us who are not experts can often do more harm than good by attempting to enter the arena of specialized controversy. But that does not mean that we have to be passive. You need the planning and the blue-prints of the experts; but they, too, are helpless and will fail not only to put their plans into execution but even to plan aright, unless they have the clear vision of the end for which they ought to plan, the wholeness of the human family, and are supported by the strong will behind them of the people to see the end realized. And that is where the ordinary man and woman have to help. You may not be able to discuss the tech-nicalities of a plan; but if you see that the end in view is not the true end, you can fight against it; and always and every-where you can, simply by being yourself a whole man or woman, spread among those with whom you come in contact a sense of what the right end is, and the urgent necessity of achieving it.

There is a further sense in which national and international societies are like individual men and women: you can ignore and repress one or many of the elements in them, and if you do, the repressed elements will sooner or later rise and take their revenge and perhaps destroy their former masters. And if their revenge is, in fact, destruction, the last state may well be worse than the first. Think of the wars between the nations, think of the yet more cruel wars within nations: at the end of them you have what one of the Popes called the "mournful heritage of hatred and revenge," the seeds of fur-ther wars. It is not only as individuals that we must die in order to be reborn. There is one thing that these years of war have made very plain: it is not the people who have been silently through the bombing of their homes and cities who, as a general rule, desire to wreak the same savage destruction on their enemy's homes and cities; and those who have been through the horrors of the concentration camp and have not been killed or gone crazy, they are not the ones who hate. They have gone beyond hatred. The thing is too big for hatred. Your armchair strategist shouts for the bombing of civilians; your sheltered critic burns with righteous indignation at the crimes of the concentration camps: these, who have known what these things are, do not shout and burn with hatred. When you have seen to the very depths of the degradation of human nature, when you have seen a vileness that is bigger than man, you cannot hate. You can only be silent, and pity, and pray. And then you can begin to say, "Out of the depths have I cried unto Thee, O Lord; Lord, hear my voice."

Then, having done that, you can begin to build, to build all over again, but still with hope. After the death, the resurrection. When you are in love you must say, "Lord, I am responsible for ever for this child"; but you can build the world only when you are in love with the world, and so of the whole world, too, you must learn to say, "Lord, I am responsible for these children." No, you are not a sovereign of a State, you are not a great leader of men, you are not a great public figure, you have no great influence in world affairs, and perhaps you think you have none at all. But you are still responsible. When the world goes wrong, it is your affair; when the world sins, it is your responsibility. You have had your part to play in the battle of good and evil; and have you played it entirely as you ought? Have you always, have you ever, been filled with the power of the Godhead to heal the blindness and the suffering of humanity? You must go down anew into the depths, and see again the face of evil, and be humbled; and if the horrors which are upon us could only bring us all to that, they would not be in vain, they would not be fruitless, and those innocents whom these horrors have robbed and made homeless and tortured to death would not have suffered without purpose. "Unless the Lord build the house, they labor in vain that build it." There was One who came to build the world anew; and He was tempted to take it by storm, to be a man of power as, having all power, He could so easily have been. But He refused because He is the Truth, and knew that only the Truth can make us free, can bring us from death into life. When you have gone down again into the depths, and seen the horror of humanity in the grip of evil, you may come again to see the heart of humanity and to be humbled before it; and you will start building afresh in the service of the Truth, and will not allow yourself to despair, for you will remember Him who went before you and in whose life and power you work, and you will remember that at the end He said, "The work is perfected," but that He said it as He was dying on the Cross.

VIII

The Making of the Church

Catholics call the Church their Mother. It is easy to smile and say, "Of course; because to be a Catholic you have to bury your own mind, believe and do what you're told, and behave like a babe in arms." It is so easy a comment that you might suspect there is something wrong with it.

Look at the life of an ordinary healthy family living in love: there are two aspects. There is the unity based on authority: the children accept the parents' right to teach them the truth about things and to tell them how they should act. But there is the other side: the members of the family are not machines but human beings; the children develop minds and wills and destinies of their own; and all together make the life of the family.

The Church, too, has its double aspect. When Christ's years of visible life upon the earth were ending, He wanted to ensure three things: He wanted to make sure that the truth—the essential elemental truths without which men cannot be restored—should never be lost or distorted; He wanted to make sure that His own power should continue to be available to men; He wanted to make sure that He Himself should remain with men. So He made the Church: to keep safe what He had come to tell us, to have the power to give us His life and power, and to have the power to give us Himself. That is one thing that we mean when we speak of

147

the Church. But there is the other side. "I am the true Vine; ye are the branches." We also mean by the Church the company of all those who believe in Christ and love Him; we mean more than that, for there are all those, so we believe, who through no fault of theirs do not acknowledge Christ's presence in His Church or even the divinity of Christ Himself, but who yet serve truth and goodness in their lives according to the light that God has given them: we do not think of them as "visible" members of God's Church, but we think of them as belonging to it, and destined one day to belong to it fully.

Let us here take only the Church that all can see: the authority, and those who accept the authority. We call the Church our Mother: are we then just babes in arms? The danger in the human family is that the children may cling too long to their mother's skirts and never grow up: they have to learn from their mother to be whole men and women in their turn; but having in that sense established their independence of the life of the family, they return to it, still to take life from it indeed, but also to give life in return. So, with obvious differences, in the Church: you need it to teach you and empower you to be a whole human being; but in the strength of that power and that truth, you are meant to enrich the life of the Church in your turn, to serve it as a whole man or woman. There is the same danger: you can choose to remain infantile if you will, you can refuse to develop a mind and a will of your own; but if you do that, you will never be fully a Catholic, you will never fully serve the Church.

But the Church claims an infallibility that no human parents could ever claim, and so the comparison breaks down? Yes, the comparison breaks down, but only in the sense that it is not a perfect parallel. What is this infallibility?

Suppose you have some very precious possession, something intimately connected with someone you love, do you fail to do everything you can to preserve it and keep it from harm? Suppose when you were dying you had some vitally important message to hand on to your descendants, would you fail to take every possible means to ensure that it should be handed on intact? And if you had power to influence directly the minds of those who came after you, so that on this point at any rate they should never forget or be muddled, would you not take it? Christ had the possession of the truth to hand on, the truth without which the human family would be lost again: would He not use His power precisely in this way, so that generation by generation these elemental truths should not be forgotten or distorted or diminished, but should remain?

In this respect we are as children, yes; but, again, there is the other side. If you think of what is handed down as simply a number of lifeless propositions, so that we read and learn and then there is nothing more to be done, of course you think of the believer as a child with its horn-book. But the object of belief is not a number of propositions but the Being of whom the propositions attempt in halting human language to tell us; you read and learn, but then you are at the beginning, not the end; you must go on thinking, praying, learning, so that you understand more and more, and always you are only at the beginning. And we are given truth and we are given life; but it was the Truth who said "I *am* the Life": you cannot separate the two things; for as you believe not in a statement but in a Reality, so the work of faith is not merely the exercise of the mind but the living of a life, the embodying of the Reality in every thought and word and deed.

And do you think that this is a thing the teaching Church

does for you? The teaching Church gives you vision and power in order that, having learnt to think and will aright, you may make your own life well.

Some people criticize the Church on the ground that it takes away freedom of thought. Other people criticize the Church on the ground that it has nothing to teach modern man that is relevant to his problems and needs, or that it lacks the courage to criticize the assumptions of modern society. It is an easy target, especially for those who will not take the trouble to examine either the nature of what they are criticizing or the implications of their criticisms.

"It takes away freedom of thought." Have they never heard of Catholic scientists and philosophers and theologians, or do they take them all for fools or knaves? Have they never heard of the development of dogma, and where do they suppose the development comes from? Of course the Church is, within a certain defined area, intransigent; yes, and sometimes harsh and apparently cruel. And supposing you alone know the truth about someone you love very much, and you find people ignorantly maligning him: do you sit placidly by, or are you roused to a fury? And supposing you find someone perverting the minds of children who are unable to defend themselves: are you silent? Do you say, "We must have freedom at all costs," and let the evil thing go on? Do we need to think of recent political examples? You cannot judge the Church's attitude here unless you understand the Church's attitude to God and the world in general. On the one side, the duty of defending the truth without which men would be lost again; on the other, the "little ones," the children who cannot defend themselves against every insidious falsehood: how, on these essential things, can it fail to be intransigent? But it will not adapt itself to the discoveries of modern science? No, and what does this mean in practice, but that as each successive scientific hypothesis becomes fashionable, the Church refuses to rush uncritically into an accommodation with it and to jettison for it the eternal truth? How very foolish it would be if it did. These critics do not stop to consider that the Church's view of humanity has been verified for two thousand years, while scientific theories are almost as fleeting and unstable as fashions in clothes. That is not a criticism of science but a recognition of the nature of science: we learn, of necessity, piecemeal.

The divine truth and power are held in all too human hands; and if you think that zeal to defend the truth turns easily into cruelty, or prudence turns easily into blind conservatism, you may be right. But do not confuse human clumsiness or frailty or wickedness with the wisdom of a divine love and care. Allow for the fact, which every Christian knows only too well, that to be a Christian is not to be automatically a saint, and that therefore, though Christ's power unerringly fulfils His purpose, we can do violence to His love of man by the way we serve His purpose. Then, hold if you will that Christ left no safeguard to His truth or any truth to be safeguarded, and that, therefore, the Church's intransigence is inexcusable; but do not hold the second conclusion unless you hold the first; and even then, you must blame the Church not for the intransigence which follows inescapably from the first assumption, but for the assumption which leads to the intransigence.

"It takes away freedom of thought." But does it? "In the Middle Ages they would not even let the people read the Bible in their own tongue." No, they preferred to teach the masses by word of mouth because they were unlettered and uncritical; but do not say that it was the Church's fault they were unlettered and uncritical. Who kept the torch of learning alight in Europe, and built up a cultural tradition which is still the basis of our own? Who built the universities throughout Europe, not as preserves for the rich and mighty as in later centuries, but for the thousands of poor scholars from every land—and were these scholars kept from the Bible, any more than from the pagan poets? Do you think they came on foot from all over Europe simply to be indoctrinated with a lifeless dogmatism? Have you never felt the thrill of this spring-time of Europe, even across the ages: the thrill of new continents of the mind discovered, and others behind them waiting discovery; the zest of the battles of wits and the rival philosophies; above all, the sense that here was not a trade, a study, something to be learned by rote, but a life into which you could plunge, a life always moving, always enlarging its boundaries, a heritage from the past but also and above all a challenge and a promise for the future?

The world has sunk low since then; and we live in times when the life of the mind means little to the bulk of the Western world; but do you think that the life of the Church is at a standstill, or that the stream of doctrinal studies which appear in half the languages of the world is no more than an endless repetition of what is already said? Do you think there is nothing in Thomas Aquinas that is not to be found in Augustine, or that the thinkers of to-day add nothing to the thought of yesterday? The central core of truth remains the same, for otherwise you would have not truth but error; but endlessly new aspects, new implications, are discerned and a deeper insight gained. This search and study of the unchanging truth is in its turn a life of love, and therefore an endless process of discovery—"pens and heads," as Milton said of a different city and in a very different context, "sitting by their studious lamps, musing, searching, revolving new notions and ideas . . . others as fast reading, trying all things, assenting to the force of reason and convincement."

And where does the impulse to add to and develop our understanding spring from? Primarily from the love of the truth itself; but also from the impetus given by the development of philosophy and the sciences, endlessly producing new ideas, new approaches, which demand the renewal of the work of comparing, sifting, judging, incorporating, that the body of truth as a whole may be better seen. Dogma is not the denial of thought but an invitation to thought. You do not add to truth by abandoning the old at the first brush of real or apparent contradiction with what is new, but by seeing whether and in what way the old is enriched and enlarged by the new. Tradition (as opposed to dead conservatism) is not a cerecloth but a living force: if you want to see the death that follows on the loss of tradition, look at the rootless suburban barbarism which calls itself modern civilization.

But the development of dogma is not the business simply of a learned minority. We are all involved. If you study the long process of evolution as history reveals it, you find that it begins from below, it begins with the common people; it begins as often as not with a new expression of religious faith or devotion, and on that there follow the controversies of theologians, and only then are these controversies finally resolved by the defensive voice of the Church as a whole: defensive because, in the heat of controversy, one or the other side will threaten, at least by implication, the unchanging truth. The truth is the life, and to live the life is to live the truth; but life is movement, and to live the truth is to grow in understanding of it: and behind the conscious rational searchings of the theologians there is always the deep intuitive sense of the eternal, the constantly deepening love-knowledge, of the Christian men and women who are living in God.

The Church, then, has nothing to teach modern man that is relevant to his needs? Do they think, these armchair critics, that we who are taught have other needs than theirs? Even if the Church said nothing of the problems which are particularly those of the world of today, would it have nothing relevant to say? Have we outgrown the age-old dreams of humanity? Have human nature and the deepest needs of human nature completely changed? The one thing necessary is still the one thing necessary, as it always has been and always will be. But the first word of truth is the word repentance, the dying of the grain of wheat: when unpleasant things are being said, it is easy to persuade oneself that nothing is being said.

And our own particular modern problems: are these ignored? If so, the life of the Church must be a fantasy life, a weaving of webs in the void. We had not noticed it, we who are appalled by the chasm between what we have learnt of what ought to be and what we have seen of what is. Social justice, sex, war, education, international life—these are things which are in the forefront of minds and consciences today; and do you think the Church has nothing to say about them? The simplest textbook of moral theology will tell you enough about usury or the immensities of marriage or the duties of ownership or the problems of war and peace to fill you with horror at the inhumanity of the world you live in.

But circumstances change, and the old books do not deal with the realities of the new age? No, but their ageless principles do. If you study the morality of war, you do not have to discover anew that the willful slaughter of the innocent is a crime: you only have to ask yourself a question of fact—is this or that new method of warfare a slaughter of the innocent,

154

yes or no? If you study the morality of modern finance, you do not have to discover anew that usury is a crime: you only have to ask whether these new financial trickeries are usury or not.

And is the Church silent even so? Does the Church fail to rebuke the modern crimes of modern societies? It is significant that on all these questions—justice, war, sex, education, world society—there have, in recent years, been special papal letters addressed to the world. If you think the Church is afraid to rebuke society, read the burning anger, the scalding condemnations of the cruelty and irresponsibilities of the rich, in *Rerum Novarum* and its successors. If you think the Church is subservient to national interests, study the consistent attitude of the papacy in time of war: remember the words of Pius X to the Emperor of Austria, "I bless peace, not war"; the words of Benedict XV, "perfectly impartial" because he must consider "not the special interests which divide" the combatants, but the "common bond of faith which makes them brothers"; and remember how a New York paper described the words of Pius XII in the present conflict as a "verdict from a high court of justice." Judge the papacy by its constant habitual policy, not by one or two controversial incidents in which its impartiality may seem to you to have broken down; and do not, when you hear that the Pope has given his blessing to a number of young men torn from their families by a dictator to be turned into cannon fodder, do not for heaven's sake read into this simple priestly duty a declaration of political partisanship.

The divine life and truth are held in the frailty of human hands; we know that. Popes are not sinless; and we do not think them infallible in anything but the most formal exercise of their official function as the voice of Christ on earth. If you say that Catholics—laymen, priests, bishops—are often mis-

155

taken in their views and blameworthy in their actions, no Catholic will contradict you. If you say that the history of the Church is a long succession of scandals, you are telling the truth, though if that is all you say, you are distorting the truth. But do not say that the Church has nothing to teach us. "Moral theology," said Cardinal Faulhaber, "will speak a new language. It will remain true to its old principles, but in regard to the permissibility of war, it will take account of the new facts." As of war, so of the other modern problems: the Pope speaks, and not only at Rome but all over the world the work of "musing, searching, revolving new notions and ideas" goes on. And again it is not just the pastors or the theologians who are involved. Development springs also from below. There is the question of the justice of the existing social order: you may not hear the verdict of the official Church unless you go and ask for it, for today the official Church cannot command attention from the world; but have you failed to hear the verdict, not in words but in deeds, of Catholic youth, have you failed to hear of the Jeunesse Ouvrière Chrétienne, the Young Christian Workers, who in their thousands—in France and Belgium especially, until the war struck them down—are a living indictment of the iniquities of our industrialism and a determination to redeem that industrialism from within? They are developing dogma, not on paper but in the toil and tears of their own lives. They are making the Church.

Yes, there are scandals, as there have always been. Yes, you can point to masses of Christians to whom all these things mean little or nothing; you can point to Christians in high places who seem to be opposing instead of helping onward the work of the Church. You can find examples in plenty of greed and cowardice and subservience; and we who see the

Church from within can paint a far blacker picture than those who view it only from without. But what conclusion can you legitimately draw, apart from what we already know, that there is evil in the world and that the cosmic struggle is fought not only by the Church but within the Church? There is only one conclusion you can draw: that Christ is not a man of power. He is infinite power: how else could His Church have gone on, and kept its doctrine undiminished and its life unquenchable, in face of these endless betrayals? But He is not a man of power: His power is real power, the power of love. He leaves us our free will. The truth must at all costs be kept, and so the divine power remains within the Church as infallible guide; the life and the power must be kept, and so there is the official Church to hand them on. But there must not be compulsion of free beings, there must not be the destruction of the divine handiwork which would result if free beings were turned into automata. The Body of Christ is the extension in history of the personality of Christ, as the child is the extension of the personality of the parents; but the best parents may find they have a naughty child, and the wisest parents expect to. So the Christian family, in its turn, must die in order to live; must begin its making of life by the doing of penance. We are all responsible.

And those who criticize from without, those who, perhaps, are partially members of the family and ought to be more: *they are responsible too.* If you criticize the Church for its lack of fullness of life and if, had you thought more deeply and with less prejudice, you would have understood better and perhaps been nearer yourself to the Church, then you criticize the Church for a failing which is your own fault. The Church is not meant to be a closed system within the larger framework of human society: it is meant to be human society. It is meant to give life and power to every man and woman; so that every man and woman can help to build up its fullness at each moment of the history of the world.

The life and the power are from God; but here too God waits upon our will. Here too, here above all, there are tensions and therefore betrayals: the tension between the false self and God, between greed for the world and poverty of spirit, between selfishness and brotherhood, between sloth, ignorance, complacency, sectarian pettiness, and the zeal and zest of the love that restores God's family. True, there are some people who reject with scorn the possibility of miracles but who themselves demand miracles the moment they begin to criticize the Church: a man's upbringing and environment may hide from him the urgency of one or other of our pressing problems, his own bent of mind may be in quite other directions, and he may be doing real service to humanity in those directions, but no, he must become aware, by some divine inspiration, of this particular problem, and be able instantly to deal with it as an expert, and his prejudices and limitations and shortcomings must fall from him as at a stroke of a wand.

We who are Christians know the injustice of many of these criticisms. But we who are Christians know, too, the scope there is for criticisms which are justified. Only, we want to make sure, we want above all to make sure, if we can, that criticisms find the right target and not the wrong one. People sometimes talk of the betrayal of Christ by the Church.[1] But there can be a terrible confusion here. There is the divine

---

[1] It is more usual to speak of the betrayal by "the churches"; but I have no right to speak of any religious communion but my own; and the Catholic Church, for us who belong to it, is necessarily "the Church," into the

side of the Church, the bringer of truth and life and power to the world, the extension in history of the life of Christ: this cannot betray Christ for it is Christ, and the truth and the life and the power are always there. There is the human side of the Church, the men and women who hold the divine life in their hands, the communion of saints which is also, however, the communion of sinners, ourselves; and we do, indeed, betray Christ, we betray the truth and the life, and in so doing we betray precisely the Church which is our Mother and through which the truth and the life are given us. You must not speak of the betrayal of Christ by the Church: you must speak of the betrayal of the Church by the Christians.

We betray the Church when we refuse through sloth or indifference or selfishness to use the power of the Church to destroy evil within us and free ourselves from the bondage of sin. We betray the Church when we refuse to grow up: when we refuse to use the power that is offered us to grow in love and vision and free ourselves from the bondage of sin; when we keep our worship at the infantile level, and confuse religion with magic, and treat prayer as though it meant filling up a blank check for all the goods we require. We betray the Church when we let love disintegrate into sentimentality, so that religion becomes an emotional self-indulgence; or when, for the love that should set out to heal the world for God, we substitute the selfishness of an isolated self-culture. We betray the Church when we think it sufficient to be busy about many things and to fulfil with accuracy our external religious duties, instead of remembering that the first thing is to be a man of vision, to be one with God. We betray the

unity of which we hope that one day all lovers of Christ will be brought by the power of the Spirit.

Church when we develop a sectarian intolerance—not the divine intolerance which will not allow the truth to be whittled down to accommodate error and evil, but the diabolic intolerance which will not admit that others, too, may know something of the truth, and love and be loved by God. We betray the Church above all by the sects and schisms which still divide the Church—and if we say that these are not our fault or our responsibility, perhaps it is the greatest betrayal of all.

We need to recall the noble words of the Papal Legate, Cardinal Pole, at the second session of the Council of Trent: that the evils which have come upon the Church and rent the Body of Christ have come "because we left the well of living waters," so that "of these evils we are in great part the cause, and therefore we should implore the divine mercy through Jesus Christ." "Consider then," he says, "the birth of these heresies which in these days are everywhere rife. We may, indeed, wish to deny that we have given them birth, because we ourselves have not uttered any heresy. Nevertheless, wrong opinions about faith, like brambles and thorns, have sprung up in the God's-earth entrusted to us. Hence even if, as is their wont, these poisonous weeds have spread of themselves, nevertheless if we have not tilled our field as we ought—if we have not sowed—if we took no pains at once to root up the springing weeds—we are no less to be reckoned their cause than if we ourselves had sowed them; and all the more since all these have their beginning and increase in the tiller's sloth. . . . If like our fathers we were suffering for justice' sake we should be blessed. But because the salt has lost its savor, we are suffering justly yet not for the sake of justice. . . . 'O Lord, to us is confusion of face, to our princes and to our fathers who have sinned. But to Thee, O

Lord our God, mercy and forgiveness, for we have departed from Thee. . . . And on us is the malediction and the curse.'"[2]

Today we pay the penalty in the very immensity of the obstacles which prevent the reunion of divided Christendom. Behind us are all the years and centuries of divergent development: it is not only that the divided communions hold different views about the truth, but that by now they have different approaches to the truth, so that the task of understanding one another is immeasurably increased. But behind this intellectual problem there is the deeper problem of the will: the legacy of the centuries of enmity and hatred and distrust; and until these evils are completely exorcized, it is useless to hope for unity of mind. And so we come—and it is one of the main themes in Cardinal Pole's address—to the primary need of repentance and humility, that the power of God may be able to work in us and through us. *Omnes nos peccavimus*: we have all sinned; and until we are all filled with that sense of sin, until we have gone down into the depths of self-knowledge and sorrow, we cannot serve the healing purposes of God, we can only resist them.

We betray the Church—and sometimes it is a subtle temptation—whenever we compromise the truth by using evil means to achieve a good end. Sometimes people say of a war, at least implicitly: "Our cause is just, so what difference does it make what methods we use?" It makes all the difference between good and evil.

You will see many different expressions of the same sort of confusion. Sometimes you find it in history—and perhaps

---

[2] *Causes of Christian Disunion*: Cardinal Pole's Legatine Address at the Opening of the Council of Trent, 7th January, 1546. With Introduction by Fr. Vincent McNabb, O.P.

not very remote history—in its crudest and most brutish form, as when men think they can serve the Church by killing and torturing the innocent; though, indeed, when they do this, it is possible that they are not trying to serve the Church at all, but using the Church as a cloak and a slogan to mislead the ignorant and the stupid. There are more subtle forms. If you try to whitewash the Church's history, you are denying the truth which the Church exists to safeguard; if you try to advance the Church's power in the world by power politics, by compromising with an evil economic or financial system, by amassing wealth as a means to power even though others are in want and penury, you are denying the poverty of spirit and the purity of spirit of Christ. It was indeed His own temptation—to establish the kingdom by Mammon and the sword; and the temptation could not bend His purpose because He knew that real power is love, and He chose the failure of the Cross and made it victory. We betray the Church whenever we forget, or pretend to forget, that real power is love.

The betrayal of the Church is our responsibility, and lies on our shoulders like a cross. The building of the Church is our responsibility too, and stands before us like a challenge. And always we must be either betraying or building: there is no neutrality. For the building is not something special that we have to do: if we are living in God it is everything that we do. Every act of betrayal, if it had been instead an act of worship and love, would have helped on the work of building. It is as simple as it is difficult. We build God's Church if we obey God's Church, responding to the life and power that are given us and so becoming holy. We build God's Church if we treasure and ponder over His truth till it takes possession of us and makes us strong and mature of mind, so that we learn

162

to see the problems and circumstances of every day as God would have us see them, and help on the endless development of dogma.[3] We build God's Church if we try in His power to become men of prayer, and so to live in Him and to be made whole.

You cannot do these things and leave the life of the Church and the world unchanged. If you never learn to pray and so to become one with God and the world, then, indeed, you may live completely enclosed in your isolation in this sense also that when you die you will leave no legacy, your life and your death will have made no more difference than the falling of a dead leaf to the ground. But the saint, not by what he does so much as by what he is, transfigures the world; and even when he dies, his life and power remain with those who come after. Here and now we enjoy the addition of life that the saints have brought us, just as we reap the whirlwind which the sinners have sown. The most secret saint in his hermitage has more power than the tyrant who can change for a time the face of the world. When Abelard fled to the forests for refuge and solitude, the students flocked out to him there: he had that which turns a great mind into a great force—the power of personality; but we have the letters of Héloïse to witness that he was not a saint, and now the power is gone and he is only a name and a legend. But when God's life builds upon this power of personality, or when, as sometimes happens, it supplies the lack of it, then you have an influence which the ages will not quench. What we are we owe largely to others; and we, in our turn, can determine largely what others will be; and the long process of receiving life and giving it goes on endlessly; so that if you today are a

[3] Cf. Appendix, 162.

saint, the holiness of others in a thousand years' time may be due to you. If you are a saint, your personality will never touch the lives of others without influencing them; by what you are you can reveal reality to them, or at least revive the thirst for reality which was dried up in them. They say of St. Dominic that he spoke only to God or of God: and do you think, then, that he was always preaching? Not at all; but if you are a saint you can talk of philosophy or science, of nature and art, of great things or small things, the making of kingdoms or the humble things and events of home, and always the breath of the Spirit will be on your lips and your words will carry like an unspoken blessing the scent of the winds that blow from the eternal hills.

We fight in the battle of good and evil, the battle between heaven and the false self. If you are a saint you will give life to an immense multitude; but your own life will for that very reason be a great victory against evil: for when the multitudes press about you and try to touch even the hem of your garment you will do the exact opposite of what the false self would do: you will send them away from you to follow their Master.

You will not be sending them away empty. *Introduxit me rex in cellaria sua:* you will be sending them to the King's store-rooms, that the hungry may be filled and be able to give others of their abundance. Have I spoken too much of the life of making, of the joy of making, and forgotten the unhappy, the loveless, the derelict? But you, if you are making the Church, it is what you are for: to see that none are left without love and happiness, none are lonely. It is what you are for; "to visit the fatherless and widows in their tribulation." It is what you are for: to feed the hungry, to give drink to the thirsty, to clothe the naked, to harbor the harborless. It is what you are for: to go out into the "streets and lanes of the city, and bring in hither the poor and the feeble and the blind and the lame"; to go out into the "highways and hedges and *compel* them to come in," that the house may be filled. Yes, there are some for whom the life of loving and making may mean only a treasure that was snatched from them, or a treasure that was never theirs; but it is what you are for: to show them that, if they live in the Church, they live in love and will be makers—will make more by humility and simple prayer and patience than by living in high places. Yes, we know that the company of Christians is a company of sinners as well as of saints; we know that we go far from the "well of living water," and cause many evils to come upon us; we know that because divinity is held in human hands, there is stupidity and ignorance and intolerance, sometimes there is much to be suffered, and sometimes there is much to give us shame; but we know that all this is ultimately unimportant compared with the charity of Christ, we know that all this is not the substance of the Church's life, we know that the substance of the Church's life is in the cry of St. Paul, that "neither death nor life nor angels nor principalities nor powers nor things present nor things to come nor might nor height nor depth nor any other creature shall be able to separate us from the love of God, which is in Christ Jesus our Lord."

If you live in the Church and try to use the power of the Church to increase the life of the Church, then the power of the Church will make you yourself whole; and in your wholeness you will help to make your family and make your world. But you will be building for a more than earthly beatitude because you will be building the city which is eternal. Here you build in shadow, you build for a future which is invisible, and so you can only build in hope. And often your plans will be wrecked and your dreams come crashing about your ears, and you will need the strength of the Rock which is Christ to give you patience and fortitude, for often it will be not the wicked who wreck but the good. You build in shadow for the sense of sin will be upon you, and the better you build the more you will see how bad a builder you are. You build in shadow because sometimes the loneliness of sin will come back upon you, and you will want to think God your enemy, you will want to be a master and refuse to be a child. You build in shadow because sometimes God will take from you even what you have built well, even what He has given you—the family you have made, the love He has given—and you will feel discarded and forgotten, as Christ felt when He was making the sacrifice of the Cross. But these are just the times when you must build most hardily and with greatest intensity of labor: for these are the times when you will build best.

If you live in the present you will not despair of the future. It is for God to give the increase. Live in the present, live in the eternity of God, even as you walk the roads of England; and the fleeting moment, which mocks as it flashes beyond your grasp, will be of infinite importance in itself though its passing will be unimportant, for you will know it as part of the ever-present; and then you will gather up all the shame and the splendor of humanity's past into the arms of your responsibility, and all the promise and all the disappointment of the future into your cupped hands held out in offering and worship. And when death has come to you, itself a fleeting moment, so unimportant, so infinitely important, the earth will still belong to you and still will look to your love and power for its making, and the Church will bless you for the life you have added to it, and there will be men to heed you better than they did when you were here, for

what the dead had no speech for, when living,
They can tell you, being dead; the communication
Of the dead is tongued with fire beyond the language
    of the living.

But you, for your part, will be no longer in the shadow but in the glory of the Light inaccessible; you will be in the City that is yours because you helped to build it; you will see Him at last as He is, and be wholly with Him; and you will have no more any mourning or weeping or any other sorrow, for all these former things will have been transmuted into happiness and peace, and you will walk with Him—together with all those you have helped to bring to Him, even until the end of the world—you will walk with Him in happiness for ever, in the cool of the eternal evening.

Appendix

The Christian doctrine of the Fall of man raises in acute form a widespread contemporary difficulty. There are many who recognize the grandeur and the validity of the Christian moral law; there are many who see beyond that, to the necessity of religion, and who would, perhaps, acknowledge the truth of what they would regard as the substance of the Christian faith; but Christians they feel they cannot be, because of the insistence of Christianity on the acceptance of dogmas which to them appear scientifically untenable and, indeed, to the mature mind of the modern West, ridiculous. What is the truth of the matter?

Let us be clear first of all about the nature of Christian morality. There is one thing you just cannot do: you cannot accept Christian morality while rejecting Christian doctrine; for the simple reason that the morality without the doctrine ceases to be *Christian* morality at all. You can retain a sort of shadow-pattern of the Christian law; you can use the same names; you can act in the same way as far as externals are concerned; but the substance of what you do is changed. And the substance is changed because both the final purpose of what you do and the spirit in which you do it are changed.

You can give to your neighbor his due, and that is to act with justice; but not necessarily with Christian justice. You can act justly from motives of pride, because you seek honor or advancement; you can act justly because you see that unless you are a just man, you cannot be a happy man; but in both these cases your main purpose is, with differing degrees of nobility, selfishness. You can act justly because you love humanity; and still this may not be Christian justice. You cannot be just in the Christian sense unless you seek first the Kingdom of God and His justice; unless your life is centered not in self nor in man but in God. Prudence, justice, fortitude, temperateness: these are virtues known to the pagans also; but *Christian* prudence and the rest resemble them less than they differ from them; for these Christian virtues are aspects of religion, of worship; they are ways of loving God; they are ways of living with God and becoming one with Him (and we can become one with Him because He is three-in-one, because the Godhead transcends even the distinction between absolute and relative, and therefore, need not remain aloof from its creation: so that in Christian morality the belief in the Trinity is essentially involved). The end is different because the end is not any earthly end however noble, but the giving of glory to God by becoming one with Him.

But the manner is different, too. The grandeur of these pagan virtues is that they are the noble qualities of the mature, independent man, the man who has made himself free. In the Christian virtues there is this; but it is only half the story. There is the man; there is also the child. "I live, now not I, but Christ liveth in me." The way to wisdom is humility; and the way to humility is the sense of insufficiency; and the way to the sense of insufficiency is the sense of sin. Every act of virtue is an affirmation of the love of God; it is also an affirmation of the fact of sin, of the need of the restoring power of God: belief in the Word made flesh, and in our need of His power and His gift of it. And even so the tale of difference is not complete; for in the virtues it is the power of God, indeed, which is operative in us, but we judge and legislate by fallible human reason; there are times when human reason is woefully unequal to its task, and when the only way to act wisely and fruitfully is to listen directly to the voice of the Spirit, the Spirit which is like the wind that bloweth where it listeth in its spontaneity and freedom, and which gives to the full Christian life its poetry and fire and carefree gaiety. You cannot have Christian morality without belief in the Holy Ghost.

Take belief in God and worship of God from morality and you soon destroy even the morality itself: we have seen it in our day and should know. Take away the first three commandments: belief in God, reverence for His name—for His power and authority, for His law precisely as His law—and worship of Him; and soon the other commandments crumble. You will have the break-up of the family, the dishonoring of parents whose authority is from God: we have seen it in our day. Then you will find that human life comes to be held cheap: the individual in his isolation loses his greatness; you find him turned into an economic unit, a political pawn; suicide a legitimate choice, murder a matter of expedience: we have seen this in our day. When you have degraded the life of the family and the immensity of the human being, there is no good reason to reverence the mystery of sex: it becomes a plaything, and adultery an agreeable and unimportant pastime. But if you do not respect a man's home, why should you respect his property at all? And you find yourself in a world of thieves: the still illegal thieving of the gangster, the barely legal thieving of the usurer and the financial trickster. And then, when all stability is gone from life, and every man is out for himself, and might is right, then, of course, the power of credit, the worth of a man's bond, goes in its turn, and civilization in any real sense, the culture of the spirit, is destroyed. And these things, too, we have seen in our day.

But you can avoid this degradation by believing in God and worshipping Him, without necessarily accepting the Christian doctrine? True, but at best you remain at the minimum; you miss that which makes morality not merely grand and noble but divine, not worthy of respect merely but worthy of love. You miss that which brings man near to God and God near to man; you see the power of God but not the pity; and it is that pity, that droppeth as the gentle rain from heaven, that gives morality its gentleness and humility and the gracious child-like quality which makes austerity lyrical.

But then, finally, why can you not believe in the divinity of Christ and in His power and His promises without at the same time having to force the mind to accept a host of other beliefs which seem not only an insult to the scientific intelligence but also completely irrelevant? Why can you not believe in the Incarnation without having to believe that we are as we are because a problematical woman called Eve ate a problematical apple?

Here we are, I think, at the centre of an acute modern problem and of a widespread misunderstanding. Many people, people who know their Jung, for example, would say of the first chapters of Genesis, "But of course it's *psychologically* true, true as a mythos expressing a spiritual condition of the human race; but to regard it as literal history is just puerile." The first point to be decided here is what exactly you mean by literal history; but behind that there lies the question: Have those who argue thus really thought out the implications of the phrase, "psychologically true": can any fact be completely and *finally* explained in terms simply of psychological processes; must not any immediate psychological explanation lead in the last resort beyond itself; or at least is it not true that an ultimate explanation in terms of a reality beyond the human psyche is something that experimental psychology can neither prove nor disprove?

This is a vast issue, of which I can do no more than touch the fringe. But I have received permission to reproduce here a letter from a non-Christian friend, a distinguished doctor whose interests have led him to the study both of anthropology and of religion. In this he raises a number of relevant points, in the discussion of which certain useful ideas may perhaps emerge. He is dealing precisely with the doctrine of the Fall.[1]

"The conception of the Fall of Man," he writes, "appears to me to entail the acceptance of the following premises: —

(1) The descent of all mankind from a single pair.

(2) That this pair lived in a state of innocence and intimate communion with God.

(3) That as a result of temptation they sinned by performing a forbidden act.

(4) That as a result of this they obtained knowledge of good and evil.

(5) That they thus lost their pristine innocence, were cut off from intimate communion with God, and became subject to death.

(6) That the offspring of the original pair inherit the acquired sinfulness of the parents, and are likewise cut off from intimate communion with God and subject to death. (The question of the Mediation of Christ and the Atonement do not enter here.)

---

[1] The *italic* letters inserted in the course of the letter mark the points picked out for discussion in the subsequent pages.

"The first two premises fall within the province of anthropology. The views now pretty well generally accepted are to the effect that the species *Sapiens* to which we belong is the only present representative of the genus *Homo*. At least three earlier species (Neanderthal, Rhodesian and Heidelberg man) are known to have arisen within the same genus but they are now all extinct. There is evidence of the earlier existence of certain allied genera; they appear however to have been rather more nearly related to certain of the apes than to man and are usually classified as distinct.

"We are therefore concerned only with the species *Sapiens* of the genus *Homo*. It may be granted as a possible though not provable hypothesis that this species did in fact originate as a 'sport' in one offspring, distinguished in certain peculiarities of the central nervous system, from a single mating within the genus. This offspring would then be Adam, the father of all mankind; and his birth, the creation. (*a*) It should however be noted that the 'sport' might just as well have been a female, in which case Eve would have preceded Adam.

"The original Adam (or Eve) is entirely hypothetical, but we do know a good deal about the very early representatives of *Homo Sapiens*; we know what tools they used and how these tools were developed; we know something of their arts and crafts and can guess at their mode of life; in this we are helped by observation of primitive races, either now or lately existing on earth, in what is so far as can be judged the same state of culture as the earlier races of man. (*b*)

"Many of these races, described by Elliot Smith as the 'food-gatherers,' do indeed live in a state of pristine innocence. They seem when left to themselves to be free of jealousy, envy, covetousness, malice and all uncharitableness. In fact so far as these virtues are concerned they do approximate to C. S. Lewis's 'paradisal man'; it is, I think, reasonable to suppose the same of the remote ancestors of the whole race of *Homo Sapiens*.

"But enviable though this state of primal innocence may, in certain of our moods, appear to us, is it to be regarded as admirable or as one to which we should wish to return? (*c*) I think the most interesting fact brought out by Malinowski and his school of anthropologists is that these primitive races have a very highly developed communal sense but little or none of individual 'personality.' Apart from the impulses arising from the stimulation of the sensations, their behavior is governed by a tradition so ingrained as to be almost instinctive; so strong is this feeling for the community that members of it may actually die if even through mischance they happen to break a taboo and thus cut themselves off from it. Of reason and the moral law, as distinct from the tribal law, they seem to have only the faintest glimmerings. If through contact with 'civilized' man they are brought to develop reason, their innocence and primal virtue soon disappear. In fact they become as gods, knowing good and evil.

"But the fact that reason is misused is no ground for eschewing it. Reason is that which distinguishes man from the beasts that perish. It is the Word (*d*) spoken of by St. John which is the light of men, and shineth in darkness and the darkness comprehends it not. All Christians, and, I imagine, many who do not profess Christianity or call themselves Christians, believe that the Word became incarnate in Christ. Reason then is the Light; in its absence is chaos, which is evil; therefore, while recognizing how faint are the glimmerings of that light in ourselves, we must regard it and cherish it above all things, for it is only by its guidance that man can attain to his full humanity, and only through the development of his full humanity that he can attempt the ascent to God.

"This development of the reason is no easy matter, and so far mankind has made but a poor fist at it; how easily he may wander out of its light has been demonstrated in many epochs and in none more strikingly than in this present. The development of the reason is a matter of struggle and endeavor but it is the only struggle really worthwhile; therefore though I may like and admire those in a pristine and inborn state of innocence I cannot accord them my full love or respect or wish to return to their state. It is on this account that Lewis's 'paradisal man,' born into and living in a state of innocence, arouses in me no enthusiasm. According to him, such a man would be like Adam walking with God. This, you will see, is where I finally part from the Old Testament story. The state of walking with God appears to me to be attainable only by struggle and endeavor, through agony and tears and bloody sweat. (*e*) Lewis's definition of the 'paradisal man' appears to me to entail irreconcilable attributes.

"The development of the reason depends upon a sense of individual 'personality.' It cannot develop until that sense appears; hence it is but feebly developed in the primitive peoples with their strong community sense but weak sense of individuality. When the sense of individuality does develop, it brings with it the potentialities of moral choice, and hence the knowledge of good and evil. (*f*)

"Evil, as you have pointed out to me, is the absence of, or separation from, God. The Fall consisted in a choice or decision to disobey, in other words to depart from, God. But my interpretation of the Fall would not be as a wrong choice by a remote ancestor in a distant past, but as an ever-persistent phenomenon in the life of man in all times, ages and places since man became man endowed with reason and therefore possessing the knowledge of good and evil. (*g*)

"The wrong choice consisted and continues to consist in acting against the moral law, in other words in shutting out God from our lives. As to how we may approach God and attain knowledge of His laws and the power to practice them—that is another question.

"I am glad to have had the opportunity of unburdening myself on this point to you for the reason that it represents one aspect at any rate of a matter which has been a good deal on my mind lately.

"You, I feel sure, realize that there is, certainly in this country and probably throughout the world, a great stirring towards religion. Men are realizing that they cannot do without it. As I expect you realize, it was for that reason that I personally sought you out. I spent part of my adolescence in a milieu in which the existence of God was at least regarded as a matter for debate; but a large part of our present generation has grown up in a climate of opinion that regards the subject as definitely closed—to the exclusion of God, and of the possibility of any values other than purely material, as wishful thinking and a sign of intellectual weakness. It is only lately that, to drag myself in, I came to realize that there is any mode of approach to reality other than through the intellect and the scientific method; I have not, I regret to say, the training to enable me to convey this to others; but it must remain my method of approach, and, in view of the hold which the idea of 'science' has upon the imagination of mankind as a whole, it offers, I think, the best method of approach for modern man. (*h*)

"But a gulf seems to be established between the exponents of the traditional religious forms and the minds of the present and oncoming generations by the prestige attaching to the scientific method. It seems to me that this gulf can only be closed if traditional religion will accept and make a part of itself the fruits of reason as gained by the method of science. Whitehead seems to intimate this in his *Adventures of Ideas*; Macmurray says it in *Freedom and the Modern World*, and more explicitly in his *Challenge to the Churches*. To me it appears that one of the principal obstacles to the closing of the gulf is the continued acceptance and teaching of outworn doctrines, dogmata or what you like, by religion as traditionally established. (*i*) I know that science also has its doctrines and dogmata, but at least they are under continual revision in the light of emergent knowledge: no one offered any serious objection to the modification of Newtonian physics by Relativity; on the contrary it was welcomed. I know that dogmata may express profound truths; I freely admit that there are mysteries entirely insoluble by the unaided reason. (*j*) But are the doctrines of Christianity presented to ordinary men and women in such a way as not to offer an affront to their intelligence?

"This question of the Fall is a case in point. I have endeavored to put to you a view which I think might be accepted by any intelligent man or woman: how far will it square with what the Churches teach on the subject? (*k*)

"The Virgin Birth is a further case in point. I remember our touching on this in the course of a discussion one night; I did not then pursue the matter; I was sure that there is some perfectly good explanation of the doctrine and I should dearly love to hear it from you; I am equally sure that the explanation would involve excursions into metaphysics into which it would be quite impossible for me to follow you. But that is no good to the common man; it is worse than no good: it is a stumbling-block and a rock of offence. If he has any smatter-

178

ing of anthropological or classical reading he will have come across the Virgin who brings forth a Son long before the time of Christ. (*l*) The symbolism may appeal to him even though he may not understand it, but as a matter of historical fact he will be unwilling to accept it—and yet such acceptance may be demanded of him as a prerequisite to his admission to the grace of Christ, the love of God and the fellowship of the Holy Ghost.

"Now that the dispersal and breaking-up of communities of all sorts, due first to industrialization and more lately and acutely to war and other factors, have had time to make their effects felt, it seems to me that men are feeling their isolation more than ever and are coming to fuller realization of the truth that we are all members one of another; (*m*) that they are feeling as never before the need for a Communion of which all those of goodwill may be members. And Maritain says: 'La Cité temporelle ne requerrait pas de ses membres un crédo religieux commun . . . et tous, catholiques et non-catholiques, chrétiens et non-chrétiens, dès l'instant qu'ils reconnaissent . . . les valeurs humaines dont l'Évangile nous a fait prendre conscience . . . se trouveraient par là même entraînés dans son dynamisme et seraient capables de coöpérer à son bien commun. . . .' What will the Churches do towards building this Temporal City? (*n*)

"Time was when it was the rigid doctrine of the various religious communities that kept men apart; but now a vast body of men and women stands outside any religious community; it is to them that the appeal must be made. Who is to do it? 'The fields indeed stand white unto the harvest, but...'"

It must surely be impossible for a Christian to read a letter such as this without being deeply moved, without feeling a

sense of shame and a determination to do something, however small, to narrow the width of the gulf that lies between.
Certainly we shall not achieve anything by trying to pretend
that the gulf is not there: we shall merely fall into it. And perhaps that is the first thing that must be said: we shall only do
a disservice to truth if we try to throw away or cover up anything which is likely to outrage not so much the mind as the
intellectual *mood* of the modern. To try to accommodate the
mind of Christianity to a prevailing mood is, in fact, to sell
the soul of Christianity, to lose the substance in pursuit of a
shadow. This, too, we have seen happening in our day. There
was a mood in which the idea of sin was regarded as an outworn superstition, and the devil a relic of medieval mum-
mery. Now the mood has changed; the world which refused
to learn from the Church has begun to learn from Jung something of the dark reality of sin and the immensity of the
power of evil. But what of those Christians who, in the mean-
time, had decided that the world was right and the Christian
tradition wrong? They find, presumably, that the whole depth
of the Christian reality has now escaped them; the divine
power to restore is meaningless to them because they have
lost the sense of the need of restoration; the sense of solidarity with a sinful universe is lost, and with it the sense of the
all-embracing infinity of the love of God: the knowledge of
the immeasurable depths of the divine pity, which alone can
fill the abyss of the human heart, is gone from them, and they
are left clutching forlornly at some long-since-exploded
hypothesis of perfectibility.

We cannot betray the truth for the sake of making it palatable to a passing intellectual fashion. But there is no need to
suppose that, therefore, our hands are tied. You can respect a
mood without truncating your intelligence to conform to its

prejudices; indeed, you *have* to respect a mood if you want to talk to the mind behind it. And what is the prevailing mood at the moment? It has been called the "laboratory mind": not the outlook and approach to reality of the scientist himself, but the assumptions and prejudices made popular by some of the camp-followers of science: the persuasion that "science is all," that if a thing cannot be dissected and explained by experimental science, it cannot exist... You must respect what there is of truth in this attitude of mind; it has within it distorted remnants of the real scientific mind: the passion for research and investigation; the refusal to accept hypotheses without scrutiny, without exhaustive testing; the deep thirst for the knowledge which is latent in the world of material things—all this is great, and greatly necessary, and if you flout it, you bring scorn on the truth you set out to serve. But at the same time, you must not confuse the gold with the dross; there is the second and equally pressing need to point out where validity ends and blind prejudice begins. You have only to invoke the simplest and commonest facts of the experience of love or of art to show how hopelessly inadequate these assumptions and prejudices are; and from that, perhaps, you can go on to show that science is but one province in the kingdom of reason, and reason but one kingdom in the continent of the mind. Then there will be the third task: to show that your reverence for science and your limitation of its validity to a confined sphere are not two contradictory things but two complementary aspects of your reverence for reason and truth as a whole: that you do not abandon the integrity and the critical spirit of the scientific mind when you pass beyond the realm of science; and that facts and truths can be nonscientific without being unscientific.

It is worth making clear to what an extent the laboratory

mind is itself unscientific. Psychology has already been mentioned: as long as we have to admit that, in Jung's words, the psyche is itself something "beyond science," something of which science cannot have complete and exhaustive knowledge, it is unscientific to claim that science can provide a complete and exhaustive explanation of its content. Ultimate explanations derived from beyond science may be true or false; but science can neither prove nor disprove them. The basis of all scientific method is never to go beyond your facts.

Again, there is a deal of unscientific argument about the Book of Genesis. The laboratory mind will first read it as though it were a laboratory book; then declare naturally enough that it is absurd; and then declare that Christians are absurd for swallowing it. "What sort of a people do they think we are?" But to read poetry, or ancient Semitic history, as though it were a modern Western textbook of biology is a most unscientific procedure which, it is to be hoped, any self-respecting Christian would eschew, having too great a reverence for reason to do such violence to it.

To read Genesis at all, you need at least to know the difference between the literal statement of historical fact, the metaphorical statement of historical fact, and pure allegory. There is a world of difference between the Book of Genesis and *Pilgrim's Progress*; but there is also a world of difference between the Book of Genesis and a modern history textbook. If I say of a soldier who fought with great bravery in Libya that he fought with great bravery in Libya: that is a literal statement of historical fact. If I say of him, "He was a lion in Libya," it is presumably a metaphorical statement of the same historical fact. If, on the other hand, I make up an entirely fictitious story of a soldier who never existed and who fought like a lion in a battle which never took place, I am using language allegorically to express some truth which as likely as not has nothing to do with firearms. When we are told in the Book of Genesis that God brought all the animals before Adam that he might name them, it is possible to interpret the incident in any of these three ways: the Catholic would not take it in the third way; but no one would take it, unless he were very silly, in the first way. No one in his senses would suppose that God (in corporeal shape perhaps, and with corporeal noises?) assembled the patient beasts in an endless orderly queue and then left the unfortunate Adam to rack his brains for names for them. But the fact that it is not a literal presentation of history does not mean that it is not a presentation of history at all. God gave him "*dominion* over the beasts of the field and the fowls of the air": that is the historical meaning; and it is a historical fact that we need to know if we are to understand our present plight.

All that is not to say that it is always easy to decide what in Genesis is metaphor and what is literal statement; far from it; but at least it becomes clear that you can read Genesis as a historical document in a real and profound sense without getting embroiled in an irreconcilable conflict with a science with which the book has no concern.

Conflict there may well be in individuals or at given moments of history, yes; but not ultimate and irreconcilable conflict. The mind and tradition of Catholicism are plain here: you have to choose between a prudence which often looks like over-caution in acknowledging the progress of science and an eagerness for the advance of knowledge which may, in fact, be imprudent. Prudence, because what is at stake above all is the faith and the happiness of the "little ones." If you are cautious and slow, you may be tardy in incorporating new knowledge in the total of truth; but if you

183

are hasty, you may find that the new knowledge, ill-digested and unwisely popularized, is leading the unlearned not so much to the new (and secondary) truth as away from the indispensable substance of the old. And that this last shall not happen is the first duty of the teaching Church. It is exciting and sometimes profitable to gamble on a hypothesis; but not when eternity is at stake. Cajetan, the fifteenth-century scholar and follower of St. Thomas, states the traditional principle of Catholic Biblical study in this connection when he says that we should take the text as literal statement of fact unless it is clear from text or context that this is not the case; and we must include among the evidence from the text itself, if we are to be faithful to the thought of Cajetan's master, the compelling force of a certitude concerning the relevant facts drawn from sources other than the Bible, sources such as science. But it must be certitude. Given the certitude that the world was not made in six days but in millions of years, it at once becomes clear from the text that the author in describing the creation is using the language of metaphor to describe historical events. Not to accept the scientific certitude here would be a treason to the truth; for truth is one.

But certitude is one thing, and hypothesis, however attractive or probable, quite another. It is the mark of the laboratory mind to treat any fashionable hypothesis of the moment as though it were an unquestionable certitude. You may think that the Church, in its guardianship of the Bible, is simply fighting a rearguard action, gradually abandoning its former positions when science at last compels it to do so, but always reluctantly, always with a bad grace. But this is, at best, a one-sided view of the situation. To insist upon waiting until scientific hypotheses are really proven is not a treason but a service to the truth; there is such a thing as over-caution, yes: but behind the facts of history as anthropology sees them, there are other questions of greater importance, and there are the millions of "little ones" in the world to whom anthropology means little but these other questions everything; they must be guarded; if you begin too hurriedly to say that this and that is "only a metaphor," they may be led to suppose (quite erroneously but disastrously) that in some way the deepest truths which lie beneath the metaphor are themselves only a fairy story. The slowness of the grinding of the mills of God can be exasperating; but our Lord had harsh things to say to those who are a stumbling-block to the little ones: sometimes we tend to forget all about the little ones.

Still, you may think that the Church is over-cautious; but, at least, do not think that when it does incorporate the findings of science and use them to interpret the Biblical text, you are witnessing a triumph of science over dogma. Nothing could be further from the truth. There is a world of difference between accepting new light on the manner in which eternal and therefore unchanging truth is presented to the mind of man and hushing up or even rejecting a part of that eternal truth because it does not seem palatable to a transitory mood. The former the Church must always do, because it believes in human reason; the latter it will never do, because it believes in truth.

But then, may not science eventually prove conclusively that to read Genesis as in any sense a historical document is to pervert its meaning, and that its purpose is not to tell us the story of a "remote ancestor in a distant past," but to describe the present state and problem of our own souls here and now? The first answer to this must be that the thing cannot ever be *proven*, scientifically, either way, precisely because the matter of discussion is beyond the realm of science. But you can legitimately ask whether the Church's position is a reasonable one, and whether, perhaps, the progress of science will not cause it to appear less and less reasonable as time goes on.

Let us begin by recalling something of what the Church's position in this context is. It might perhaps be put very briefly by saying that it is *reasonable* to argue thus: the universe is either ultimately unintelligible or ultimately intelligible; if the former, there is no point in further discussion, for discussion is meaningless; if the latter, then it is reasonable to suppose a correspondence between the nature of things (including their ineradicable natural desires) and their actual destiny. The witness of humanity throughout the ages seems to show that the deepest desire of human nature is for a fulfilment which goes beyond the finitude of created things, a fulfilment which can only be found if the spirit of man can in some way enter into relationship with God: that is what all the symbolism of humanity is about. There is the theory according to which the human being is at length absorbed into deity, but this entails not the fulfilment but the loss of personality; there is the theory of fulfilment by a real relationship; and this means that deity must include (and therefore go beyond) both relative and absolute—an apparently insoluble difficulty which is met, however, in fact, by the doctrine of the Trinity. But how is this union to be achieved? Is it something which man can achieve for himself unaided? There is the presence of evil in us, the tug away from God, the might of Mammon, the mystery of iniquity in the world as a whole: it is reasonable to see this presence of evil as due to the action of a will other than the divine will, and the only hope of an at-one-ment of man with God in the power of the Word made flesh—made flesh because it is the nature of man

186

itself that evil has warped and weakened and made helpless and in need of rebirth.

But is not the gradual evolution of *Homo Sapiens* from lower forms of life itself a sufficient explanation of the evil with which we have to contend within ourselves? Perhaps; though I think there is a *quality* as well as an immensity about the evil with which experience makes us familiar which such an explanation would leave untouched; there are, too, such awkward phenomena as the sense of sin, which would be hard to explain and harder to explain away. But in any case, where does the evil originally come from? It is surely reasonable to think that eventually you are driven back upon an act of will, an act of rebellion to a right order—in other words to an original sin. It is at least as a shadowy intuition of some such reality, and its concomitant of a restoration of fallen nature by divine power, the divine power of a mediator, that the secular dreams and the secular myths of humanity have meaning.

And then, given the reality of the Incarnation of the Word to restore the world, it is of vital importance to realize that the rest of the Christian teaching hangs together organically in dependence upon it: the Church with its sacramental system precisely as the extension of the life and power of Christ through the ages; the Christian idea of virtue, not as the unaided progress of a self-sufficient *Homo Sapiens*, but as the humble effort to accept and be faithful to a power greater than himself.

That idea of humble acceptance of a power greater than humanity goes to the root of the matter. Even were there no evil in man, could he achieve his divinely offered destiny—to be one with God—unaided? We believe as Catholics that he could not. We believe that, by the primal sin, human nature lost its wholeness; but we believe that it lost something very much greater than that. We believe that the ultimate destiny of man is something that he cannot achieve by his own power, and could not achieve even though human nature were in itself whole and unspoiled, precisely because it is an infinite destiny, and therefore cannot be achieved at all unless the power is given by God. That power is itself a "*super*-natural" life, a sharing in the life of God. And it was *that* life, above all, that was given by God and then lost by the Fall; and it is that life, above all, that we mean when we speak of the restoring of man.

This, too, you cannot attempt to prove; but you can say that it is not unreasonable. And, indeed, it is plainly very reasonable, once you accept the idea of a finite being with an infinite destiny—and to speak of that destiny as at least the desire and the dream of the human heart is to do no more than record the facts of experience.

Let us here note a point of importance: it is the point marked (*g*) in the above letter. It is surely wrong to regard the Fall as *either* a wrong choice in a remote past *or* a persistent phenomenon in all times and places since man became endowed with reason. The Church does not reject the latter interpretation in favor of the former: it affirms them both. It affirms them both because it makes a distinction between two uses of the word primitive which the writer of the letter does not make. The argument in the letter could be summarized by saying: The choice of evil depends on the presence of reason, but reason is not primitive, therefore the choice of evil is not primitive. If the spirit of man were as much a part of the evolutionary process as his body, the argument would hold; but in the Christian view—a view which again, on other grounds, is at least reasonable—it is not. Spirit is being of an altogether different *kind* from matter, immortal, incorruptible, the "participated likeness" of the divine nature, coming, therefore, straight from the hand of God; and therefore, quite apart from the question of man's sharing in the gift of divine life and power, there is an abyss of difference between what we mean by primitive as opposed to civilized and what we mean by primitive in the sense of preceding the Fall.

So much of the letter depends on this distinction that it may be useful at this point to return to it in detail and add brief comments on the particular points raised.

(*a*) The word "creation" is used primarily to denote the creation of the universe in the embryonic form from which it has emerged into its present shape; it is possible for a Christian to hold that there came a point in the process of evolution at which the body of a particular individual of a species became capable of being "spiritualized" or humanized by union with spirit, and thence of being "divinized" by receiving the life and power of God, and so of beginning the long history of mankind: this spirit, being outside the evolutionary process, is in its turn a creation, as is every spirit coming into the world—which is why parents are called "ministers of God's omnipotence," human procreation and divine creation going together to produce the whole human being. The presence and acknowledged dominion of the immense power of spirit in the human personality, "ordering all things sweetly" within it, would presumably spiritualize, refine, the flesh itself; but the Fall destroyed the order; it robbed man of the gift of divine life because the primal sin was itself precisely the refusal to accept that life; and it diminished even the natural power of spirit, so that reason becomes obscured and flesh degraded; there is a sinking back to something nearer the purely animal level, which perhaps explains the supremacy of the herd-consciousness in primitive tribes to which the author of the letter refers.

Must we as Catholics hold that the human race is descended from a single pair? Certainly the language of both Old and New Testaments and the tradition of the Church make it difficult, to say the least, to think otherwise; and scientific opinion on the point seems to be so uncertain and so divided that the practical difficulty can hardly be said to have arisen. Perhaps from the nature of things it never can. But I think it might be legitimate to argue that, supposing for a moment the theory of several Adams were to be scientifically demonstrated, it would be a question of reinterpretation rather than an insoluble opposition between faith and science. For the substance of the Genesis story, and therefore of the theology dependent upon it, would stand. We believe that by a primal human sin human nature lost the life of God and became depraved in itself also, so that all those who share in that nature share in its defects, and stand in need of divine restoration. St. Thomas remarks that had Adam not sinned, but one of his descendants, then *this* sin would have meant the corruption of human nature, in which all the descendants of this sinner would have been involved. Suppose the human race to have begun simultaneously in several places, it only means that you would have to suppose either that some of these families remained sinless, and their posterity also (for which there is little enough evidence in the world), or else that all of them fell and that human nature in all of them was corrupted, so that for all of us still the fact of sin and the need of divine restoration remain. But now: —

(*b*) We cannot, on the Christian view, claim to learn much about paradisal man from the mode of life of primitive tribes, for the simple reason that what we know of men we call primitive applies by hypothesis only to man after the Fall. Paradisal man was no doubt primitive in the sense that he lacked the amenities of civilization; but he certainly cannot have been primitive in the sense of being lacking in individuality. Innumerable things which we know would have been unknown to him; but on the other hand, the intellectual power of an undamaged human nature would be of a strength and keenness unknown to us; and to imagine a human being sharing the life of God and yet remaining unaware of his individuality is impossible. If we search for some sort of parallel of the paradisal existence, we shall find it not in the lives of primitive tribes as we know them, but in, say, the idyllic conditions, unselfconscious yet wise, simple yet mature, of ancient Greek myths. The "food-gatherers" may live in a state of pristine innocence so far as the social virtues are concerned—and, indeed, in so far as Mammon means little to them, this is likely to be so. But

(c) that is far from saying that their condition is admirable and that we ought to return to it. To begin with, we should not even wish to return to the actual social *conditions* of paradisal man: all the labor of practical reason, the discovery and practice of the arts and crafts, the gradual evolution of civilization, lay before him; and some of this work we have done even in spite of the presence of evil, and cannot wish to retreat from it. But that we should think the life of the primitive tribe a paradisal state is very much less acceptable, precisely because of their lack of the sense of individuality, the sense which in Adam, who "walked with God," must have been very strong. The integral man, whether we are speaking of history or of ideals, must be the man-child: child because of his docility to divine power and wisdom, but man because of his maturity and independent personality; and what could be more strongly and deeply felt in a human spirit not absorbed in but united with God than the sense precisely of independent personality? We shall not regain our integrity by concentrating on the child at the expense of the man; but neither shall we regain it by attempting to return to manhood at the expense of the child. That is why

(*d*) we must not think of the Word as meaning simply the reason of man; human reason has made a sorry mess of the business of living; there is greater wisdom than that. And again, it is reasonable to think that if God is ready to restore, He is ready to instruct; and that the teaching authority of the Church is an organic element in the whole economy of restoration. But it remains true that

(*e*) we can learn to walk with God only through agony and tears and bloody sweat. Even for paradisal man, the state of being worthy to walk with God was dependent upon his effort, as is shown sufficiently by the fact that in the event he failed and fell. In our case it is more than that; there is the heavy bias to evil within us, the need of repentance, the burden of the sense of sin; it is only out of the depths that we can cry to the Lord.

(*f*) Again, it is making an unjustifiable identification of primitive tribal man with integral unfallen man to say that the primitive cannot choose evil until the sense of individuality is developed, and to apply this to the Genesis story. In the first place, where the primitive is concerned, the fact of the taboo itself shows that while, no doubt, the moral sense is a very crude one it is a moral sense, a sense of good and evil; and the fact that the taboo can be willfully broken is evidence of the possibility of moral choice. Then, as reason develops, there is a greater and greater development of the power of choice; but the emergence of this power is not to be identified with the acquiring of the knowledge of good and evil in the Biblical sense, where it means, not the acquiring of abstract knowledge or practical experience in themselves, but the attempt to attain knowledge in the sense of autonomous power—"ye shall be as gods"—the power to legislate, the power to decide for oneself what is right or wrong instead of listening to the voice of the divine wisdom.

Now it is just that attempt to legislate which seems to many of us to find expression in the determination of the laboratory mind to decide for itself by scientific method not only what is right or wrong but what, throughout the whole realm of knowledge, is true or false; it is in this that we are bound to recognize the worst effect of the "hold which the idea of science has upon the imagination of mankind as a whole" (*h*)—though indeed we should be far from agreeing that it is accurate to speak here for mankind "as a whole." On the contrary, it is surely good for modern Western man to be told just what other parts of the human family think of him. To many races at the present time he appears—as he would have appeared to most civilizations, if not all, in the past—as a naughty child playing with mechanical toys which he cannot control, and missing almost entirely the real meaning of life and the real business of living. Mr. Middleton Murry has remarked, "A child with a child's force is a comely thing; but a child with the strength of a turbine is a monstrous and dangerous thing. How much spiritual progress is required before mankind can be trusted with the physical forces even now at its command is probably not merely incalculable but unimaginable."[2] The bulk of mankind must laugh at us if it does not

[2] *Heaven—and Earth*, 26.

cry, for thinking that we are leading the forward march of humanity when all the time we are spending our strength on secondary things and forgetting the *unum necessarium*, the one thing without which all these are not only of minor importance but positively dangerous. In particular, the scientific method is so obviously irrelevant to many of the most important things of life which all men accept, that it is strange that the laboratory mind should accept them while at the same time affirming in argument that it will accept nothing unless science vouch for it: they are living, these upholders of the laboratory mind, an irreconcilably double life; and apparently do not know it.

We should not do the same. There are other methods of approach to reality, yes; and perhaps the writer of the letter is correct in saying that these are at the moment the best for modern man. But it should be made plain that this nonscientific approach to reality is not an unscientific approach to reality. It should also be made plain that so far from being a substitute for reason and the rational statement of revelation, they must on the contrary be guided by them. Otherwise there is likely to be goodness of heart and will but mental chaos. Some at the present time, in view of the obvious bankruptcy of the laboratory mind, are devoting themselves to this search for reality untrammelled either by reason or by revelation. On this point the Church has to meet two contradictory attacks: they cancel out. On the one hand it is assailed on the ground that it fetters or condemns mysticism in the name of a rational theological orthodoxy; on the other hand, that it does violence to scientific truth by sanctioning the vagaries, the nebulous dreams and visions, of the mystics. In reality it does neither. So far from condemning contemplation, it teaches that contemplation, the vision of God, is the very purpose of life. But it is quite aware of the psychological dangers of a mysticism uncontrolled by the certitudes of reason and faith; it labors under no delusions about the difference between contemplation and psychopathic delusions; and so far from encouraging deluded visionaries, it submits all claims to extraordinary mystical graces to the most searching examination. If a thing is non-rational, it may well be true; but if a thing is irrational, it cannot be true.

There are mysteries entirely insoluble by the unaided reason (*j*); and it is precisely because they are insoluble by reason that you cannot expect the substance of the Church's teaching about them to change. You can say, *post factum*, that the mystery of the Trinity is adumbrated in a thousand ways in human experience; but you could not have discovered it, unaided, from human experience, nor can you expect that reason will ever completely explain it. In other words, it remains outside the realm of rational experience; and therefore no new facts or truths which reason can bring to light will affect its validity. That is where religious mystery differs from the many unexplained facts of nature: the latter remain mysterious to us until, but only until, we find the facts which provide a key to them; the religious mystery is a mystery *in itself*, in itself it is "above reason," and therefore it is no use hoping that when further facts come to light it may cease to be one. Dogma does indeed develop; but only in the sense that we can come gradually to see more clearly the content and the implications of what is revealed. A scientific hypothesis becomes outworn (*i*) as soon as new facts disprove it or a more probable hypothesis takes its place; but a statement which is not based on reason in the first place cannot become outworn because of subsequent rational discoveries.

All that is not to say that the way in which dogma is *stated* cannot change or develop. The roots of the superstitious fear both of metaphysics and of religion on the part of the laboratory mind lie far back in the past; but the situation is immensely aggravated by more recent history, by the fact that since the break-up of the unity of human knowledge, religion and science have for the most part gone their separate ways, until at the present time they speak an almost entirely different language. (The increasing specialization and isolation of branches of knowledge today is multiplying this difficulty enormously; it might, perhaps, be asked in passing why the language of religion should be expected to accommodate itself to that of science any more than the language of science to that of religion. What is really needed is a *common* language, intelligible to both sides.)

Had Christendom continued to develop as Christendom, as a unity, theology and science would have developed together instead of drifting further and further apart in their modes and moods of thought. As it is, we have to accept the difference of approach and the differences of language. On the side of theology, we have at least to insist that the object of our belief is divine fact and not propositions about divine fact: we believe through a creed, not in a creed; we have to insist that the formularies of faith do express something of the divine fact if they are read aright; that they cannot by the nature of things express it all, and that the same facts can be expressed in different ways; but that it is worth making an effort to penetrate the meaning of the significant formularies for the sake of the realities which they signify.

There still remains, however, the question of historical events such as the Virgin Birth (*l*), which in the Catholic view are inseparably connected with the self-revelation of the Godhead, and which we are, indeed, required to accept as historical fact. I think that some of the difficulty of accepting such events as historical might be, at least, diminished if they were, in fact, viewed as a part of the total revelation of God. We believe as Catholics in the reality of matter; we believe that the primal sin had its effect in the material world in general and in the human body in particular, and that the evil which it wrought in human nature as such is handed on from generation to generation through the human body; we believe on the other hand that the divine restoration of man is accomplished also through matter—first through the humanity of Christ and thence through the instrumentality of the sacramental symbolism. It is surely reasonable, then, to hold that if the continuing power of evil in the world is to be broken by the introduction of divine power in the person of the incarnate Word, that introduction itself will *break* into the sequence of human reproduction whereby precisely the evil is conveyed from age to age. The Redeemer from sin cannot Himself be subject to the power of sin. Nonetheless, the idea of such a miraculous birth remains a stumbling-block to the common man? I do not see that it should. To the laboratory mind, yes; but not to the scientific mind or the common-sense mind. With parallels to the Christian story in ancient mythologies, I have attempted to deal in preceding pages; I cannot see that there is any good reason for regarding the historical truth of the story as impossible on scientific or rational grounds. We know something of the power of mind over matter; we know something (though far less than the east) of the power of the spirit to defy material limitations, from thought-transference or clairvoyance to the most uncanny manifestations of psychic power of a Tibetan mystic. Where some of these things, at least, are concerned, we are ready, even we of the modern western world, to admit that psychic power is power of a superior sort to material energy and capable therefore of dominating it; and if once we recognize this fact, neither the Virgin Birth in particular nor miracles in general should cause us intellectual embarrassment, for miracles are only unusual *examples* of it, though the power here is the power not of the human psyche but of God. "Stated in terms of law, miracles give the mind great pain. We can hardly bring ourselves to think of the 'suspension of law' or 'interference with law.' Yet if we use the word 'law,' miracles can be called only a suspension or a violation or an interference. Now every interference seems an impertinence, every suspension a failure, and every violation a crime. In great part therefore the prejudice against miracles rests on our unhappy use of the word law. If, however, we state miracles in terms of force, almost all the great hardships of thinking pass away. For nothing is more common in science than the conflict of forces. Indeed, dynamics is to a large extent but the science of conflicting forces and of their resultants. If there is a 'law of nature' in this matter of forces, it is that the greater force shall have its way. . . . Stated in terms of force, a miracle is the normal; any other result would be the exception. Every day the modern man sees without protest force meeting and modifying force. . . . Let the modern mind, in its philosophic moments, state the problem of miracles in terms of force, and its indignation will be unbegotten."[3]

How far then will the above letter square with what the Church teaches? (*k*) It will square with what the Church teaches in so far as it affirms that sin is a present problem in the mind and heart of man. It will not square in so far as it seems to make no admission of man's need of divine power to

[3] Vincent McNabb, O.P.: *On Miracles*, 11–12.

overcome the evil within him and make the choice of good; and it is perhaps because of this omission that it finds it difficult to see the Christian revelation as historically true as well as psychologically true. For the two things hang together. Christian revelation is an organic unity. Without the power of God we are helpless; but it is through the historical Incarnation of the Word that we receive the gift of the power of God.

We are helpless: this too, perhaps, is a stumbling-block. Are there not innumerable men and women outside the Church who lead good and noble lives, who choose the good and reject the evil? The answer for us Christians is complicated by the fact that we are far from supposing that the gift of divine power is limited to those who formally belong to the community of Christians. But, in any case, do not the words of St. Paul remain true, that even when we wish to choose aright, we in fact do the thing that we want not to do? Reason unaided is not enough; free will unaided is not enough; Enlightened Man is as much a myth as Economic Man. We most nearly approach the ideal of humanity when we fully apprehend and acknowledge the fact that of ourselves we are helplessly in the bondage of sin—for, until we do that, we are steeped in the ugliness of pride and complacency.

It is true that God might have arranged the restoration of man in a way that would be private to each individual, and perhaps in a way which the Gospel story or something like it would present in purely symbolic form. There is, indeed, something very attractive to the modern mind in such a possibility: a feeling of freedom from the fetters of a too closely defined and too exacting belief, a feeling that one would thus be free to seek in one's own way the God who had declared His accessibility, instead of being forced to conform both to a fixed standard of doctrine and to a social framework of religious life. But I think if we go deeper we find that the loss would far outweigh the gain.

In the first place we should only know the mercy and love of God by hearsay: we should miss the heart-melting immediacy of the *fact* of the Supper and the Cross. We should miss the guidance of the continuing voice of Christ; and the way of the private mystic is strewn with many dangers by reason of the essential obscurity of the dark night. We should miss the strengthening support and consolation of the sacraments, as visible manifestations of the fact that God is visiting His people. We should miss something else. At first sight it is the purely internal and non-institutional religion which is worship "in spirit and in truth"; traditional orthodoxy which externalizes and materializes the truths and processes of the spirit. But if we look further, it is not so. Perhaps the essential historical element in Christianity is given us also precisely to bring us back from materialism—that materialism into which all civilizations may be doomed otherwise to sink by way of the search for comfort, power and material efficiency. Spirituality is not in the ignoring of the flesh, but in the restoration of it. If you ignore the existence of matter in theory, you must bow to the degradation of matter in practice, as the Manichees did. Only by accepting it, its need of restoration and God's use of it in His work of restoration, can you hope to spiritualize it. But God's use of it always and everywhere depends upon the historical event: the Word was made flesh.

There is something more that we should miss if the Christian story were no more than a symbol. We are members one of another. (*m*) But why? Because we are restored to God our Father, not each in isolation, a separate individual, but all together as brothers of the Word made flesh. The private mystic runs the danger of pride: the physical aloofness of isolation is apt to become the spiritual aloofness of superiority and self-sufficiency. If men are feeling their isolation more and more, it is surely because the fellowship of the Church has ceased to be a reality to them. The natural bonds of family and nation are not enough; it is also on the very deepest levels of all that we need to feel we are a community, the family of God. But here we find ourselves once more coming back to the unity of revelation, the fact that we must "all speak the same thing," as St. Paul begged his followers to do. Without at least some measure of unity of mind there is no deep unity of heart, and we cannot be a real community until we think alike about the ultimate meaning and purpose of life.

They find us intransigent as well as old-fashioned, those who glance superficially at our doctrines and make less effort than the writer of the above letter to understand why we hold what we hold.

To say that a philosophical statement, still more a religious statement, is old-fashioned is silly: it can only be true or false. Who ever heard anyone say that Plato is old-fashioned? Will anyone dare to say that Christ is old-fashioned? And if they say that not Christ but our mode of belief in Christ is old-fashioned, do they sufficiently consider that here, too, the word is equally irrelevant, that it is intellectual moods that come to be and pass away, while the word of God which is the Word of God stands unmoved, the Beauty ever old and ever new?

And so to say that we are intransigent is to misunderstand us sadly: how shall they expect us to change the truth when even God Himself cannot change the truth since it is Himself? They might recall the wise words of Reinhold Niebuhr, about those who in attempting to adjust religion to the "mind" of modern culture found themselves involved in

201

capitulation to its thin "soul." Let us confess with shame that we, for our part, have made too little effort to repair the damage of centuries of increasing estrangement; but we must make it clear from the start that not even to gain the whole world could we tamper with the soul of truth—for then we should be gaining the whole world not to truth but to falsehood.

What will the Church do for the building of the temporal city? (*n*) Perhaps it is just through the work that is now being done for the building of the city that Christians and non-Christians may begin to come closer together, and that there may be a beginning of the most important building of all, the recovery of the unity of the family. For when we begin to talk of the needs and rights and duties of the common man, when we begin to speak not in the abstract but in the concrete of social justice and of the other virtues which give order and beauty to social life, when we begin anew to elucidate the practical meaning of the brotherhood of men: it is then that we find we are largely on common ground—and we are on common ground because we are on Christian ground.

We have to show convincingly that we hold to these things not in spite of but because of our belief in God and His mysteries; and how can we better set about it than by showing that they are indeed the inevitable *result* of that belief, and would not exist without it? This spirit of brotherhood, which may be latent and smothered by Mammon but which, as the crisis of war has shown, is far from being destroyed, this spirit is the glory of the Western world—a glory which should cover a multitude of its sins. But the whole of the Western tragedy is in this: that it has despised and rejected the *unum necessarium*, the religious life of worship and prayer, for the sake of social action and material progress, not realizing that that action is healthy and beneficent and up-building only when it is precisely the overflow and expression of prayer and worship—a prayer and a worship which are themselves social, which preserve mankind's unity of mind, which are rooted in faith and charity, and so lead to the love and service of the human family.

It will be a tragedy, indeed, if those outside the Church who are led to realize the emptiness of the uncontemplative life and the shallowness of the laboratory mind set themselves to become men of prayer while rejecting altogether the life of action, forgetting the glory of the Western heritage which is social charity. They will fall from the error of the West into the error of the East; it is not thus that we rebuild the world. M. Maritain has written very wisely: "This activism and pragmatism [of the West] are so to say the catastrophe of something which is very great indeed, but which has been jeopardized by the spirit of separation from God: the catastrophe of that generosity of heart, that eagerness to give and to communicate to others, that sense of a superabundance of being, which come from charity and from holy contemplation overflowing into action. Whereas it has to be asked whether the impassible contemplation of the East . . . which is the fruit . . . not of the descent of the uncreated Love but of the ascent of the energies of the soul struggling for a deliverance to be gained by force of an invented method and technique . . .—it has to be asked whether this does not in its turn betray in the realm of spirit itself a sort of pragmatism incomparably more subtle but which none the less shirks the witness which God expects of humanity."[4]

[4] *Questions de Conscience*, 153.

The fields indeed stand white unto the harvest... We are not unaware, we Christians, that an apostolate which does not begin in humility and contrition can only be a mockery of the Master. But there must be effort also on the other side. The laboratory mind—and perhaps we are most of us in some degree infected with it—is the result not of science but of superstition and prejudice: the refusal to see what may lie beyond the narrow confines of a self-imposed limitation of the mind. There can be little progress until that willful refusal—so different from a real intellectual difficulty—has been overcome. The Christian faith is indeed a "hard saying." Some are inclined, without sufficient investigation, to limit the hardness to the Church's dogma: to say that they are ready and anxious to believe in Christ, if only the Church did not make belief in Christ so difficult. But it is the words of Christ Himself that are a hard saying. Nor are they tender to the pride which would attempt to decide the truth for itself and in conformity with man-made prejudices; for it is through this pride that day by day the tragedy of the Fall is re-enacted, and day by day mankind refuses again to walk with God. "Except you eat the flesh of the Son of man and drink his blood you shall not have life in you. . . . Many therefore of his disciples hearing it, said: This saying is hard, and who can hear it? . . . And he said: Therefore did I say to you that no man can come to me unless it be given him by my Father. After this, many of his disciples went back and walked no more with him." Always we want, like doubting Thomas, to have visual or tactual proof of the invisible and impalpable: it is not until, like Thomas, we see the stupidity of confusing the material with the immaterial that we can learn humility of mind and cry with Thomas, "My Lord and my God."

www.ingramcontent.com/pod-product-compliance
Lightning Source LLC
Chambersburg PA
CBHW032055080426
42733CB00006B/276